Simply Descartes

Simply Descartes

KURT SMITH

SIMPLY CHARLY
NEW YORK

Copyright © 2018 by Kurt Smith

Cover Illustration by José Ramos
Cover Design by Scarlett Rugers

All rights reserved. No part of this publication may be reproduced, distributed, or transmitted in any form or by any means, including photocopying, recording, or other electronic or mechanical methods, without the prior written permission of the publisher, except in the case of brief quotations embodied in critical reviews and certain other noncommercial uses permitted by copyright law. For permission requests, write to the publisher at the address below.

permissions@simplycharly.com

ISBN: 978-1-943657-35-3

Brought to you by http://simplycharly.com

Contents

	Praise for *Simply Descartes*	vii
	Other *Great Lives*	ix
	Series Editor's Foreword	x
	Preface	xi
	Acknowledgements	xv
1.	Descartes's System: The Big Picture	1
2.	Mind	25
3.	The Search for Truth and Certainty	41
4.	Body	64
5.	Physics and the Mechanization of Life	76
6.	Human Beings	92
7.	Descartes's Legacy	111
	Suggested Reading	115
	About the Author	118
	A Word from the Publisher	119

Praise for *Simply Descartes*

"*Simply Descartes* is the perfect one-stop-shop for all matters Cartesian. Smith presents Descartes's entire system from the ground up, building from metaphysics and epistemology to physics and morality. In some ways, he even goes one step further than the master himself for, with the benefit of hindsight and of the work of leading scholars, Smith reconstructs the system in a neat, orderly, clean and concise way, extracting the disparate pieces from Descartes's many works scattered over many years. For those seeking entry into Descartes, or into philosophy in general, as well as for those seeking a refresher on this foundational thinker, you can do no better than this book."
   –**Andrew Pessin, author of *The Irrationalist: The Tragic Murder of René Descartes* and Professor of Philosophy at Connecticut College**

"Descartes said philosophy should begin by making no assumptions. He would be happy with this book because it makes no assumptions about what the reader knows, and then builds a clear and accurate picture of the most important thinker in modern philosophy."
   –**Thomas M. Lennon, author of *The Plain Truth: Descartes, Huet, and Skepticism* and Emeritus Professor of Philosophy at the University of Western Ontario**

"*Simply Descartes* is an impressive work on several levels. Professor Smith is simultaneously engaging, accessible, scholarly, precise, and bold both in scope and interpretation. Situating the Cartesian philosophical and (what we now call) scientific system in historical and intellectual context, Smith offers an outstanding overview of everything from Descartes's metaphysics and epistemology (and even some of Spinoza's and Malebranche's) to his underdeveloped, but still present, moral theory. This is at once a fabulous introduction to Descartes himself as well as the scholarly debates surrounding the interpretation of Descartes's work."

–**Kristopher Phillips, Assistant Professor of Philosophy at Southern Utah University**

"In this inviting little book Kurt Smith, author of the acclaimed *Matter Matters*, introduces the systematic thought of René Descartes. In easily understandable, non-technical language, Smith makes it abundantly clear why Descartes is regarded as one of the most important thinkers of the past and why his thought is still relevant in many respects. I heartily recommend *Simply Descartes* as a non-academic entry into this fascinating philosopher that is backed up by reliable scholarship."

–**Alan Nelson, Harold J. Glass Professor Director of Graduate Studies The University of North Carolina at Chapel Hill**

"Kurth Smith's *Simply Descartes* is, simply, the real Descartes, with all the intellectual rigor, made accessible to the non-philosopher. It is a first-rate intellectual biography that exposes the systematicity of the Cartesian program and can help almost anyone understand why 'I think, therefore I am' is worthy of being philosophy's most famous quote."

–**Seth Bordner, Assistant Professor of Philosophy at the University of Alabama**

Other *Great Lives*

Simply Austen by Joan Klingel Ray
Simply Beckett by Katherine Weiss
Simply Beethoven by Leon Plantinga
Simply Chekhov by Carol Apollonio
Simply Chomsky by Raphael Salkie
Simply Chopin by William Smialek
Simply Darwin by Michael Ruse
Simply Dickens by Paul Schlicke
Simply Dirac by Helge Kragh
Simply Einstein by Jimena Canales
Simply Eliot by Joseph Maddrey
Simply Euler by Robert E. Bradley
Simply Faulkner by Philip Weinstein
Simply Fitzgerald by Kim Moreland
Simply Freud by Stephen Frosh
Simply Gödel by Richard Tieszen
Simply Hegel by Robert L. Wicks
Simply Hitchcock by David Sterritt
Simply Joyce by Margot Norris
Simply Machiavelli by Robert Fredona
Simply Napoleon by J. David Markham & Matthew Zarzeczny
Simply Nietzsche by Peter Kail
Simply Proust by Jack Jordan
Simply Riemann by Jeremy Gray
Simply Sartre by David Detmer
Simply Tolstoy by Donna Tussing Orwin
Simply Stravinsky by Pieter van den Toorn
Simply Turing by Michael Olinick
Simply Wagner by Thomas S. Grey
Simply Wittgenstein by James C. Klagge

Series Editor's Foreword

Simply Charly's "Great Lives" series offers brief but authoritative introductions to the world's most influential people—scientists, artists, writers, economists, and other historical figures whose contributions have had a meaningful and enduring impact on our society.

Each book provides an illuminating look at the works, ideas, personal lives, and the legacies these individuals left behind, also shedding light on the thought processes, specific events, and experiences that led these remarkable people to their groundbreaking discoveries or other achievements. Additionally, every volume explores various challenges they had to face and overcome to make history in their respective fields, as well as the little-known character traits, quirks, strengths, and frailties, myths, and controversies that sometimes surrounded these personalities.

Our authors are prominent scholars and other top experts who have dedicated their careers to exploring each facet of their subjects' work and personal lives.

Unlike many other works that are merely descriptions of the major milestones in a person's life, the "Great Lives" series goes above and beyond the standard format and content. It brings substance, depth, and clarity to the sometimes-complex lives and works of history's most powerful and influential people.

We hope that by exploring this series, readers will not only gain new knowledge and understanding of what drove these geniuses, but also find inspiration for their own lives. Isn't this what a great book is supposed to do?

Charles Carlini, Simply Charly
New York City

Preface

A guy walks into a bar and drinks like there's no tomorrow. Near closing time, the bartender says, "I think you've had enough." The guy replies, "I think *not!*" (*poof!*) The guy disappears. This joke, and others like it, play off of a phrase famously associated with French philosopher René Descartes: *I think, therefore I am.*

Understanding Descartes and his place in intellectual history are important—the origin of lame jokes aside. His work inspired a new way of looking at things, ushering in what today we refer to as the *modern* period. In fact, Descartes is affectionately called the first modern philosopher. Although you may have only recently become acquainted with his name, you very likely hold some of the views that he is responsible for having introduced into intellectual discourse—including the belief that you and your mind are one and the same thing; the belief that your mind is only temporarily related to your body and can survive "death;" the belief that your mind is more than capable of acquiring the truth independently of any authoritative social institution; the belief that "living" bodies are machine-like; the belief that all geometrical problems can be translated into algebraic form and solved *via* the rules of algebra—to list only a few.

Descartes (pronounced *Day-cart*) was born in 1596, in La Haye, France. His mother died roughly a year after his birth. His father, a magistrate, sent Descartes and his brother and sister to live with their grandmother. At about 10 years of age, he entered college at the Jesuit school in La Flèche. After graduating, he studied at the law school in Poitiers, then joined the Dutch army of Maurice of Nassau, Prince of Orange. During his time in Breda, where he served, he met Dutch philosopher Isaac Beeckman, who rekindled in him a deep interest in mathematics and physics (then known as *natural philosophy*), such interests having originated when a student at La Flèche. This not only inspired Descartes to author a short treatise on music, which focused on the mathematics of sound, but also a large work that he originally titled Le Monde (The World).

As Le Monde approached its printing date, Descartes pulled it from the presses, having learned of the Catholic Church's condemnation of Italian philosopher Galileo Galilei. He was imprisoned for adapting the Copernican model of the solar system, which was contrary to the Church's teachings. That was around 1633. In Le Monde, Descartes said that he too had embraced some of Galileo's controversial views. He figured that the same fate that befell Galileo could also happen to him.

Descartes spent the rest of his philosophical career, if we can call it that, reproducing some version of Le Monde. His first attempt resulted in the Discourse on the Method, published in 1637. This work included a brief autobiography (from which we learn of his initial interests in mathematics and physics as a young student), a brief account of how he took his system to be grounded, and three "scientific" texts–the Geometry, the Optics, and the Meteorology. Some claim that these three scientific essays were versions of the material originally included in Le Monde. The Discourse turned out to be quite popular. He then turned his focus to writing an intense examination of the ground of his system–the Meditations on First Philosophy. Although akin to the Discourse, the Meditations, published in 1641, goes into much greater detail as to how one must proceed when setting out to discover the ground of his system.

Descartes returned to the proverbial drawing board and authored the Principles of Philosophy, published in 1643, which highlighted the physics portion of his system, though Part One gives a brief run-through of the arguments introduced in the Meditations. Description of the Human Body, written about 1647, was the start of a reworking of the Treatise on Man, the latter very likely also originally included as part of Le Monde. And, The Passions of the Soul, Descartes's final work, finished around 1649, extends his system into taking a closer look at the psychology of man, where the makings of a moral theory lurk.

The structure and order of his work align, though not perfectly, with how philosophical systems of the period were presented to readers—logic and metaphysics, physics, biology, human anatomy and physiology, human psychology, human social structures, culminating ultimately in moral and political theory. Descartes said nothing about social structure, and barely scratched the surface with respect to moral theory, tidbits of which are found in the *Passions*. And he said almost nothing about political theory. In this book, we'll take a careful look at Descartes's philosophical system—the whole kit and caboodle. We will aim to get the "big picture," and see how everything hangs together.

Here's the end of his story. In 1649, Descartes set out for Sweden to tutor Queen Christina. He was charged with teaching the Queen philosophy, a task that he seemed not to have enjoyed since the sessions started at five in the morning. Some foreboding things occurred at the opening of the new year, one of which was Descartes's friend, Hector-Pierre Chanut (1601-1662), coming down with a nasty respiratory infection. Chanut recovered and would go on to become the French Ambassador to Holland. So, his story ended well. Descartes helped Chanut get through his health crisis, but wound up ill himself. Now, the odds are that he simply caught whatever virus Chanut had. But some have suggested that something more sinister was afoot and that Descartes, and maybe even Chanut too, had been poisoned. Although in early February there seemed to be light at the end of the tunnel with respect to recovery, things took a turn for the worse, and Descartes died early morning on February 11, 1650. Sixteen years later an envoy from France, Hugues de Terlon, arrived in Stockholm to recover his remains. He secretly exhumed the body, put it in a copper coffin, and brought it back to Paris.

There's a wonderfully macabre story about how Descartes's skull was allegedly stolen on the way to France. The *Musée de l'Homme* (Museum of Man) in Paris, is now home to Descartes's alleged skull. The story is that Swedish chemist Jacob Berzelius had read in the newspaper that it was up for sale. He purchased it. But American philosopher Richard Watson, who has held the skull in his hands, suggested that it is more than likely that of a little girl, and not that of a man in his mid-50s (Descartes died at around fifty-four years old). Museum curators disagree, of course. Besides, among other things, the front of the skull bears this inscription (in Latin): *This small skull once belonged to the great Cartesius* (Cartesius is the Latinized form of Descartes).

We cannot be certain that the skull in question belonged to the great philosopher. What we do know for sure is that his work has transcended centuries and is still influential today.

In the book that follows, when citing Descartes's writings, I refer to the now-famous 11-volume collection, edited by Charles Adam and Paul Tannery (AT). And, whenever possible, I use the English translations (three volumes) of John Cottingham, Robert Stoothoff, and Dugald Murdoch (CSM), and the third volume including translations by Anthony Kenny (so, volume three is CSMK). I place citation information in parentheses in the body of the text, the AT and CSM (or CSMK) volumes cited by volume and page number.

Kurt Smith
Bloomsburg, PA

Acknowledgements

I would like to thank *Simply Descartes*' publisher, Charles Carlini, who approached me about writing this book. I was delighted and honored to do it. The view presented in this book is the culmination of more than two decades of focused study on René Descartes and his philosophical work, though I suspect that this can be traced back even further, to my first early modern philosophy course at UC Irvine with Robert Sleigh, Jr., who in those days would spend some of the winters as a visiting scholar in sunny Southern California. The greatest influences on my thinking about Descartes—scholars and friends who have inspired and influenced me—include (in alphabetical order) Roger Ariew, Seth Bordner, Ken Brown, Jill Buroker, Vere Chappell, Patricia Easton, Dan Garber, Geoffry Gorham, Paul Hoffman, Nick Jolley, Anthony Kenny, Tom Lennon, Steven Nadler, Alan Nelson, Larry Nolan, Calvin Normore, Donald Rutherford, Tad Schmaltz, Lisa Shapiro, Ed Slowik, and Margaret Wilson. I'd be surprised if we couldn't find portions of this book that each would vehemently reject. But the fact remains that the view here was born from my encounters with these wonderful minds. It is to these unwitting partners in crime that I dedicate this book, though they'll no doubt hate huge hunks of it. But it's my book, so what are they going to do? Last, but certainly not least, I thank my editor, Helena Bachmann, whose thoughtful and careful editorial suggestions made the book a better read.

1. Descartes's System: The Big Picture

In the *Preface* to the French edition of his *Principles of Philosophy* (1647), Descartes wrote:

> Thus the whole of philosophy is like a tree. The roots are metaphysics, the trunk is physics, and the branches emerging from the trunk are all the other sciences, which may be reduced to three principal ones, namely medicine, mechanics and morals. (AT IXB 14; CSM I 186)

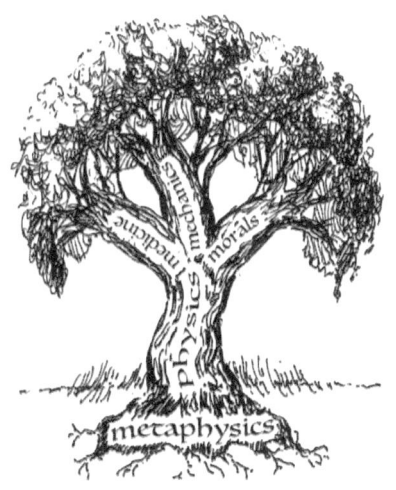

This image is helpful in better understanding Descartes's insight into how human knowledge was ultimately structured. It says something about the relationships that the various sciences have to one another. At bottom was the science of metaphysics. Like the roots of a tree, it grounded and fed all the other sciences. Next was the trunk, representing the science of physics. From physics, three principal sciences emerged—medicine, mechanics, and morals. Of course, the flipside of this was to think of the latter three sciences as being underwritten by physics, and physics as being underwritten by metaphysics. Given that the relation is transitive, the three principal sciences must be understood as being underwritten by metaphysics.

Metaphysics

The term "metaphysics" has a long history in philosophy. Today, it denotes an area of philosophy that focuses on theories of *reality*—on theories of what *is*. Included in metaphysics is what is sometimes called an "ontology": a theory of *being*. Even in terms of everyday, ordinary life we find the connections between the commonsense notions of *reality*, what *is*, and *being*. To be sure, talk of being and reality makes metaphysics sound like physics. But it isn't. Physics presupposes certain notions established in the metaphysics, notions that are formulated prior to physics—notions like *substance, mode, quality, event, cause, effect, motion, law, being, existence, body, time, space, impetus, origin*, and so on; notions that early modern natural philosophers (some of whom were later called *physicists*) in turn presupposed in their reasoning and in their explanations.

An ontology isn't solely an artifact of academic philosophy. It is found hard at work even in everyday, ordinary life—our very language expresses an ontology. When being taught how to communicate with others, you were introduced to an ontology, regardless of whether your parents or teachers understood it to be such. Consider the simple statement:

> The ball is blue.

In ordinary usage, this statement would presumably refer to or pick out some state-of-affairs in the world. You very likely call such a state-of-affairs a *fact*. You also probably believe that if the above statement picks out a fact in the world, the statement is said to be *true*. On the other hand, if it fails to pick out a fact, the statement is said to be *false*.

The statement is a linguistic item; it is a piece of *language*. The fact is an ontological item; it is a piece of *reality*. Truth and falsity, then, emerge, as they do above, from our noting the relationship between a statement and a fact. Of course, not every statement is made true by the existence of a corresponding fact. Some statements—definitions, for example—are true, but not because of some fact. But the statements of interest to us at the moment are those that are said to be true because of some fact. This is an ancient theory of truth. We find it expressed as early as in the works of Aristotle (384BCE-322BCE). In philosophy, the term "epistemology" denotes the area of study that focuses on theories of knowledge. As you might expect, since truth and falsity are constituents of any theory of knowledge, epistemology includes a study of theories of truth and falsity, too. Thus, truth and falsity are epistemological items. We'll look more carefully at Descartes's epistemology in Chapter 3. Right now, we will stay focused on working out a more general picture of Descartes's *system*, the ground of which is established in his metaphysics.

As with most statements, the above one ("The ball is blue"), can be analyzed into its constituent parts. The word-phrase "The ball" is the *subject* of the sentence; the word-phrase "is blue" is the *predicate*. As the statement picks out a fact in the world, its constituents, the subject and predicate, also pick out items of the ontology—in this case, a *thing* and a *quality* or *property* that this thing possesses. The thing is the *ball*, and the quality or property that it is said to possess is the property of *being blue*. Notice that the "is" in the statement—"The ball is blue"—isn't the "is" of identity. That is, we're not saying that the ball is identical to being blue. If we were saying that, then the sky, which is also blue, would be identical with the ball. Rather, the "is" here is the "is" of predication. We can make this a bit clearer by replacing "is" and emphasizing the relationship: The ball *has the property of* being blue.

The ontology is revealed in your learning that typically the things denoted by subject-terms are "more real" in some important sense than the things denoted by predicate-terms. For example, the ball is thought to be able to remain even if we changed its color. So, if we painted the ball red, it would still be the same ball as before, but now red. If it were your ball, for instance, and someone painted it red, that change wouldn't upset the fact that it is still your ball. If we destroy the property blue in this case, then, where we "destroy" this instance of being blue by painting the ball red, we don't destroy the ball itself. But the property of being colored is not like the ball. If we destroyed the ball, whatever properties it possessed would also be destroyed. This shows that there is an asymmetric ontological relationship between the ball and any of its properties. Generally speaking, we can say that the properties of a thing depend for their existence on the existence of the thing in a way that the thing doesn't depend for its existence on the existence of any of its properties. So, there is a lot to be said about something as simple as the sentence "The ball is blue."

It would seem, then, that a simple fact isn't so simple after all. It has constituents. Considering the case under discussion, as just noted in the previous paragraph, the constituents of a simple fact are a *thing* and some *property* possessed by that thing. In metaphysical terms, the thing is referred to as a *substance* and the property is referred to as an *attribute* (but in addition to *attribute*, *property* and *quality* are also used). This is sometimes referred to as an Aristotelian *substance-attribute* ontology, since we find it famously worked out by Aristotle himself. This would've been the ontology very likely taught to Descartes when he was a student at La Flèche.

Descartes's ontology is a version of the substance-attribute ontology. He ultimately believed in the existence of one and only one actual substance, which was an infinite being with no beginning or end. Within the context of religion, this being is typically considered to be a god—or in terms of Christianity, as Descartes understood and practiced it, *the* God (with a capital "G"), where it was said that there was only one (unlike many of the religions of the ancients, three of the major world religions—Judaism, Christianity, and Islam—rejected the view that there were many gods).

A substance, a genuine substance, existed on its own, without the help of anything else. No *thing* other than God meets this condition—or at least this was so according to Descartes. Even so, he noted that we could use the term "substance" to refer to things that weren't substances strictly speaking. But, as he said in the *Principles*, we'd have to keep it in mind that we're now using the term differently than when speaking about a substance proper. (*Principles*, Part I, Arts. 51, 52; AT VIIIA 24-5: CSM I 210) Descartes posited that there were exactly two kinds of finite substances, which, as just noted, are not substances strictly speaking, since they cannot exist entirely on their own (they require God's concurrence), but they can be called *substances* insofar as they can exist independently of one another.

According to Descartes, the two kinds of finite substances that existed are *mind* and *body*. Although he recognized several attributes, he said that there were only two principal ones, which were essential to each kind of substance. The principal attribute of mind was *thought* or *thinking*. If something thinks, it is a mind; and, if something is a mind, it thinks. The principal attribute of body was *extension* (in length, breadth, and depth—that is, it was extended in three dimensions). If something is extended, it is a body; and, if something is a body, it is extended. Here, the notion of being solid or impenetrable wasn't essential to body. "Empty space" was just as much a body in Descartes's view as was any "solid" thing—both were extended.

Descartes wrote that the principal attribute is *how* the finite substance is made intelligible to you. So, when conceiving a body, you *must* be conceiving of something that is extended. Being extended is simply what it is to be a body. If you removed extension from your conception, so to speak, nothing would remain in your idea of body for you to think about. You'd have the idea of nothing at all (or, put differently, you wouldn't have an idea of anything). The same would go for mind. When conceiving a mind, you must be conceiving of something that thinks. Thinking is simply what it is to be a mind. If you removed thinking from your conception, nothing would remain in your idea of mind for you to think about.

Descartes employed a technical jargon to make clearer the difference between a finite substance and its principal attribute. He said that they are only *conceptually* distinct. This means they are distinct only in *your* taking them to be distinct, but that distinction is only in your mind. Technically speaking, we cannot clearly conceive them apart from one another, which amounts to saying that neither can exist independent of the other. "Superman," for instance, refers to the being who hails from the planet Krypton, but so does "Clark Kent." Although we might take them to be distinct beings, Superman and Clark Kent are one and the same being, despite the fact that Lois Lane and others *take* Superman and Clark Kent to be distinct things. Given that "Superman" and "Clark Kent" name one and the same thing, in every world in which we find the thing denoted by "Superman" we'll find the thing denoted by "Clark Kent."

Likewise, you won't find extension, for instance, just floating around in the cosmos minus the finite substance of which it is the principal attribute. You won't find a naked, attribute-less finite substance just floating around either. Still, you might think you can *take* them as separate things, as when you *say* that extension is the principal attribute of an existing substance. Here, it looks like you're talking about two things—an attribute and an existing substance—but you're really talking about only one thing. Descartes was so confident of this connection that he wrote in the *Principles*: "If we perceive the presence of some attribute, we can infer that there must also be present an existing thing or substance to which it may be attributed." (*Principles*, Part I, Art. 52: AT VIIIA 25; CSM I 210) In other places, he used the term "presupposes." So, in his view, an attribute presupposes an existing finite substance, which is why you can infer from your perceiving an attribute that you're perceiving an existing finite substance.

But there's more.

Descartes suggested that *modes* are instances in which attributes are manifested in the cosmos. In this context, the term "mode" means *a way of being*. Shape is a mode. It is a mode of the attribute extension. In being a mode, shape is a way of being extended—it is how an instance of extension is manifested in the cosmos. Size is also a mode of extension. You can easily see how shape and size are related modes—both are modes of the same principal attribute. In Descartes's lingo, both share a *common nature*. When you consider a mode as being distinct from the attribute or from the existing substance of which it is a mode, you've made a *modal* distinction.

Additionally, Descartes said that when you consider one mode apart from another, you've also made a modal distinction. Concerning mind, for instance, Descartes noted that doubting is a mode of thinking. It is an instance of thinking—or it is how an instance of thinking is manifested in the cosmos. If you considered an instance of doubting as being distinct from the mind that was engaged in doubting something, or you considered this instance of doubting as being distinct from an instance of affirming or denying, you'd be making a modal distinction. Likewise, if you considered doubting as being distinct from shape, you could be understood as making a modal distinction.

Descartes was confident in the metaphysico-logical relationship between a mode and the principal attribute it "modifies," writing in the *Principles* that each mode *presupposes* an attribute. In light of this, he said, "Everything else which can be attributed to a body presupposes extension, and is merely a mode of an extended thing… For example, shape is unintelligible except in an extended thing…" (*Principles*, Part I, Art. 53: AT VIIIA 25; CSM I 210). The same, of course, would hold for mind—doubting is unintelligible except in a thinking thing. You can see how this might support the view that from your being aware of some mode, you can infer the attribute it modifies. Still, Descartes said that since doubting presupposes the principal attribute thinking, and shape the principal attribute extension, where thinking (mind) and extension (body) can exist independently of one another, you'd be better off calling that a *real* distinction. He suggested that two things are *really* distinct (as opposed to being *modally* or *conceptually* distinct): if we can conceive them (their natures) independently of one another. The only two items in his ontology that meet the real distinction criterion are mind and body. We can conceive what a mind is independent of what a body is, and vice versa. This is why casting the distinction between doubting and shape as a *real distinction* might be better than casting it as a modal distinction. The reasoning here is that since doubting and shape presuppose the principal attributes—thinking and extension, respectively—and thinking and extension are really distinct, then ultimately doubting and shape can exist independently of one another.

In holding that exactly two kinds of finite substances exist in the cosmos, Descartes is said to be a metaphysical *dualist*—where "dual" means *two*. Sometimes he was specifically called a *mind-body dualist*. Here are a few basic claims that constitute Descartes's ontology:

- **Modes presuppose some principal attribute (either thinking or extension).**
- **Attributes presuppose some existing finite substance.**
- **An existing finite substance presupposes an existing infinite substance.**

Just to be clear, we need to keep in mind that the big difference between a finite substance and an infinite substance is that the former, a finite being, isn't a "substance" in the same sense as the infinite being. Remember that, strictly speaking, only God, or the infinite being, is a substance, since it exists independently of any and all other things. Although they can exist independently of one another, finite substances like mind and body cannot exist on their own, independently of all else. Descartes posited that they are *created* beings and, as such, they depend on the thing that created them. In fact, in order for them to remain, that is, to continue to exist, their existence must be underwritten by something "more real" than either of them. This more fundamental or more real thing is God, the infinite being. This is behind the third claim above: *An existing finite substance presupposes an existing infinite substance.* Above, we referred to this relationship as *concurrence*–finite substances require God's concurrence in order to exist and to continue to exist.

God is said to have no beginning and no end, which is one way to express the sense in which God is infinite. There are "negative" ways of describing an infinite being. But Descartes adopted the more traditional theological view that God is an infinitely powerful (omnipotent) and infinitely knowing (omniscient) being. These are "positive" ways of describing an infinite being. Such a being cannot not be; or, put another way, such a being *must* be. So, questions about what kick-started God or what keeps God in existence are rendered meaningless in Descartes's system.

Lastly, in support of claim three in our list above, Descartes argued that although the word "infinite" may look like other constructed "negative" words, like "immoral" or "impossible," it is importantly different from them. With respect to these latter words, we begin with a positive stem, like "moral" and then attach the negative prefix "im." By attaching the negative prefix, we denote the opposite of the positive stem. But "infinite" isn't like this at all. To be sure, it looks as though we have taken the positive stem "finite" and slapped on the negative prefix "in." But in doing so, we are simply denoting the opposite of the finite. Descartes said:

> And I must not think that, just as my conceptions of rest and darkness are arrived at by negating movement and light, so my perception of the infinite is arrived at not by means of a true idea but merely by negating the finite. On the contrary, I clearly understand that there is more reality in an infinite substance than in a finite one, and hence that my

perception of the infinite, that is God, is in some way prior to my perception of the finite, that is myself. (Third Meditation, AT VII 45; CSM II 31)

What he likely meant here is that the *finite* is the negation of the *infinite*, where the infinite comes first, and the negated-infinite, the finite, comes second. This is a sense in which the infinite might be taken to be prior to the finite (in the same way that *moral* is prior to *immoral*). As he also argued, one might think that we simply "build" the idea of the infinite by adding together, so to speak, our ideas of finite things. That wouldn't work, he contended, since the best that you could do is to construct an idea of a *potential* infinity. That is, the best you could do is produce an idea of bigger and bigger things, so to speak. You could never construct an idea of an *actual* infinity. (AT VII 47; CSM II 32) You could never produce an idea of something that couldn't get any bigger.

Descartes examined his idea of himself, which represented him as a finite substance. His analysis of this idea ultimately revealed that it "includes" as constituent elements the infinite, where this has been "limited" in some sense. The finite, in other words, is constructed from the infinite, where by limiting this infinite being, a finite being is the result. This is another important sense in which the infinite is prior to the finite. In a letter to his friend Claude Clerselier (1614-1684), Descartes wrote:

> I say that the notion I have of the infinite is in me before that of the finite because, by the mere fact that I conceive being, or that which is, without thinking whether it is finite or infinite, what I conceive is infinite being; but in order to conceive finite being, I have to take away something from this general notion of being, which must accordingly be there first. (Letter 23 April 1649, AT V 356; CSMK III 377)

Using Descartes's notion of presupposition, we might say that insofar as the infinite is prior to the finite, whereby being prior the latter is constructed out of the former, finite being, or the idea of it, *presupposes* infinite being. We thus have a line of reason that supports our third claim on the above list, namely that *an existing finite substance presupposes an existing infinite substance.*

Formal Being

As suggested in the previous section, Descartes inherited from his teachers an Aristotelian metaphysics. Nevertheless, although he employed some of the terminology of what he had learned, he tweaked things here and there, and so he didn't mean exactly what his predecessors had meant by certain terms. One view that Descartes inherited drew a distinction between *being* and *existence*. The being of a thing was the *what* of the thing. For example, as noted above, he said that extension was the being of a body; it was that which accounted for a body's being the kind of thing it was. Remember, extension was what Descartes took to be body's principal attribute—it was what made a body a *body*. Thinking was the being of a mind; it was that which accounted for a mind's being the kind of thing it was. Thinking was mind's principal attribute—it was what made a mind a *mind*.

For the moment, in an attempt to make things clearer, let's just focus on the notion of body. In cases of ordinary sensory experience, we might say that we're aware of more than just *body* or just *a body*. Although the following aren't Descartes's examples, they nevertheless can serve to make things clearer. When you look up toward the sky, you see the Sun. That's a body. Its principal attribute is extension. But it is also exhibited in your sensory experience as having a specific shape and size. You look over to your glass of iced tea and see an ice cube floating in the glass. That's a body, too. Its principal attribute is also extension. It is also exhibited in your sensory experience as having a specific shape and size, a shape and size that are different from those exhibited to you in your sensory experience of the Sun. So, the Sun and the ice cube, in being bodies, share a common principal attribute—extension in length, breadth, and depth. Where they differ is in their respective shapes and sizes. They differ with respect to their modes.

Of course, the sensory experiences of both the Sun and the ice cube exhibit to you more than just shapes and sizes. The sensory experience of the Sun exhibits to you something that is also yellow and hot; the sensory experience of that ice cube exhibits to you something that is also white and cold. Descartes accepted all of this. Sensory experiences are like that. They exhibit *bodies* (plural) that appear to be very different from one another, their differences expressed in terms of shapes, sizes, motions, colors, smells, feels, sounds, and the like. In an early work, the *Rules for the Direction of the Mind* (c. 1628), Descartes referred to these items as *simple natures*. So, *extension* is a simple nature, *shape* is a simple nature, *color* is a simple nature, *hot* and *cold* are simple natures, and so on. Not only are our sensory experiences constituted of these simple natures but, as he told us in a later work, the *Meditations on First Philosophy* (1641), when we imagine something, we employ these simple natures; our dreams are even constituted of them. (*Meditations*, First Meditation: AT VII 20; CSM II 13-24)

Even so, as just noted, all bodies, insofar as they are such, share a *common* nature: extension. Minds, of course, insofar as they are minds, also share a common nature: *thinking*. There appears, then, to be no essential difference between bodies—all have the same nature. Likewise, there appears to be no essential difference between minds—all have the same nature. Philosophers who followed immediately after Descartes and had adopted some version of his system, like the 17th-century Dutch philosopher Baruch Spinoza (1632-1677), took bodies like the Sun and the ice cube to be only modally distinct beings. Since they shared the same nature, they could not be conceived completely independently of one another (for whether conceiving the Sun or the ice cube, you must conceive each as being extended, so you'd be conceiving *two* things with the *same* nature), and so consequently they cannot be said to be *really* distinct. So, according to Spinoza, there is only *one* body and lots and lots of modally distinct "bodies," which are nothing more than the one body "carved up" by various modes. Thus, the Sun is a modal being, the ice cube is a modal being, and so on—each is simply an instance of the one body. Whether or not that was Descartes's view is still a matter of contention among scholars. But lots of scholars are fascinated with Spinoza's take on Descartes's system, so it is worth a brief mention here. But let's get back to *being* and *existence*.

The point thus far is that the *what* of a thing—whether the Sun or the ice cube—was traditionally taken in the Schools to be the property or set of properties that accounted for a thing's being the kind of thing it was. Sometimes this was referred to as a thing's *essence* or *nature*. As you can tell, Descartes took there to be only two kinds of things and so only two essential properties: extension (for body) and thinking (for mind). Descartes's teachers, many of whom had advocated for a version of Aristotle's view, took there to be more than just these two kinds of things. For them, there were the elemental kinds of bodies: water, fire, earth, air. Each had its own distinctive essence: water was essentially cold and wet; fire was essentially hot and dry; earth was essentially cold and dry; and air was essentially hot and wet. From various (proportional) combinations of these elements emerged all other kinds of things: rivers, dirt, iron, coal, rubies, trees, apples, roses, lions, human beings, and so on, where each *kind* of thing was defined by some set of essential properties. So, the essence or nature of a thing was an account of its *being*; it was an account of *what* it was.

Now, whether or not a thing (a being) *exists* was another matter altogether. At least this was the view of Descartes's teachers. We can easily imagine a winged horse. Imagining this winged horse is accomplished by composing an idea that exhibits a thing with whatever properties are required for something's being a horse, whatever properties are required for having wings, and so on. These properties would constitute this thing's essence or nature or express this thing's *being*. Knowing the being of this thing answers the question: *what* is this? That said, we can also opine that such a being does not *exist*. Here's where things get tricky. There is a sense in which we can say *what* something is without having to say *that* it is. This suggests that there must be some difference between a thing's *being* and a thing's *existence*. Something can have (possess, exhibit, manifest, etc.) *being* and yet not *exist*. Again, just to be clear, this was the sort of thing that Descartes's teachers believed. What we'll see shortly is that it isn't clear Descartes believed this too.

Something that exists is said to be *actual*. This much Descartes adopted from his teachers. To claim that something exists was to say that it is an *actual* thing. So, when claiming that the winged horse does not exist, you are saying that it is not an actual thing. In this case, it is simply a fabrication of your imagination (where, in Descartes's terms, you have combined some number of simple natures)—so perhaps we'd agree that it is a *possible* thing, since we can imagine it, but we'd very likely agree that it wasn't actual. There are no winged horses flying about. We could say that the winged horse exists *in your mind*—that is, its existence depends on your mind. So, if you're no longer thinking about it, the winged horse would no longer *be*. But this would only serve to muddy the waters, for if we insisted on talking like this, we'd now have to make sense of the difference between somethings existing *in your mind* and somethings existing, but *not* in your mind. To keep the waters clear, if a being is actual, its existence does not *depend* on your (or on anyone's) mind. So, in this sense, the winged horse is not actual. Descartes suggested exactly this way of understanding *actual* in the First Set of Replies to the *Meditations*. (*Meditations*, First Set of Replies: AT VII 102-03; CSM II 74-75) (You might wonder whether *your* mind is actual in this sense, since it cannot exist independently of itself. But since it doesn't depend on some other finite mind, Descartes would say that that counts as being *actual*).

If we used Descartes's earlier terminology of *simple natures*, we might say that a thing's essence is constituted of at least one simple nature. Although Descartes's teachers recognized all sorts of essences—the essence of a piece of iron, the essence of a rose, the essence of a lion, and so on—Descartes recognized only two fundamental essences: extension (for body) and thinking (for mind). Nonetheless, it's worth noting that he did say with respect to geometrical shapes, such as triangles and squares, that they have *true and immutable natures*. (*Meditations*, Fifth Meditation: AT VII 64-65; CSM II 44-45) But even here, all such natures would have a fundamental nature in common—namely, extension. What he did not recognize were the various natural kinds that his teachers recognized. So, Descartes didn't seem to think that the Sun or the ice cube had *essences* that made them instances of being a *sun* or an *ice cube* per se. As noted earlier, it was the result of sensory experience that such "kinds" were ever brought to mind, and then wrongly taken to be actual kinds. The Sun and the ice cube are members of the same kind—body.

As we'll see in Chapter 3, Descartes developed a method for making our ideas clear and distinct; an important result of applying his method showed that for the most part the objects exhibited to you in sensory experience, like the Sun, are obscurely and confusedly exhibited. The Sun is nothing more than a body, whose essence is to be extended in length, breadth, and depth. It has a shape, which is spherical, it is very large size-wise (relative to the size of the Earth)—at least this is what a clearer and more distinct idea of the Sun (understood as a *body*) would exhibit to us. He contrasted this sort of idea with the obscure and confused sensory idea of the Sun that exhibits the Sun as being flat, circular-shaped, smallish in size (you can block it with your thumb), yellow, hot, and so on. (*Meditations*, Third Meditation: AT VII 39; CSM II 27)

With the above views now on the table, let's see if we can make Descartes's views on *being* and *existence* a bit clearer. For starters, Descartes held that there are two distinct kinds of reality or being—*formal reality* and *objective reality*. He would've in all likelihood learned of such concepts when a student at La Flèche. In the First Set of Objections to the *Meditations*, its author, the Catholic theologian Johannes Caterus, pressed Descartes on his use of such concepts. He strongly suggested that Descartes's employment of them didn't square with how such concepts were taught in the schools. (AT VII 92-3; CSM II 66-7) Descartes replied that regardless of how these and other concepts had been or were being taught in the schools, his own use of them was certainly clear enough for a reader to understand what he meant. (AT VII 102; CSM II 74-5) But the point is that the concepts, and the terms used to denote them, were well known to Descartes's readers. In this chapter, we'll focus on *formal reality* (or *formal being*, as it is sometimes called). In Chapter 2, we'll discuss objective reality, and how it relates to formal reality.

Descartes likely meant the following when speaking of formal reality:

Formal reality is the kind of reality a thing possesses insofar as it is an actual thing.

The Sun, understood as an *actual* (instance of a) body, possesses formal reality. To say that the Sun is actual is to state that it exists independently of your (or anyone else's) thinking of it. Of course, we're being careful here to note that the Sun is not being taken in this context as the hot, yellow disc in the sky, as exhibited in sensory experience, but as *a body*, whose essence is extension, wherein being a finite body (or an actual *instance* of body) the Sun will also possess a particular shape, a particular size, and so on. Pegasus, however, our winged horse, is not actual. It does not exist independently of your (or anyone else's) thinking of it. Consequently, Pegasus does not possess formal reality.

As we'll see in Chapter 3, when doing philosophy in what Descartes believed was the proper order, he considered the possibility (but only as a philosophical exercise) that body doesn't (or individual bodies like the Sun don't) exist. He noted that even if we allow for such a possibility and we doubt the existence of body (or bodies), when doing philosophy in the proper order we will nevertheless arrive at the insight that our doubting such a thing, which is an instance of thinking, presupposes that we exist. To put this in terms of the *Meditations*, the insight amounts to our noticing that when conceiving the attribute *thinking*, we are compelled to affirm that the thing that thinks *exists*. To put this in terms of the *Principles*, when conceiving the attribute *thinking*, we are entitled to infer an *existing* substance—the thing to which the thinking is attributed. (ATVIIIA 25; CSM I 210) This is behind Descartes's famous claim made several years before the *Meditations* and *Principles*, in the *Discourse on the Method* (1637): "I am thinking, therefore I am (or I exist)"—or perhaps more familiarly said: "I think, therefore I am." Once our ideas are clear and distinct, he said, the same holds for body—for a thing whose principal attribute is extension. When conceiving the attribute *extension*, we will be entitled to infer an *existing* substance. The being of body and the being of mind entail their existence. Both, in other words, are *actual* beings, and as such, both possess formal reality.

Descartes took there to be different "levels" or "degrees" of formal reality. For example, a mode was "less real" than a finite substance insofar as the level of formal reality possessed by the mode was less than that possessed by the finite substance. Descartes told us that the formal reality possessed by a substance's modes is derived from the formal reality possessed by the substance. This is just another way of saying that modes are less real insofar as they depend on their being or existence on the being or existence of the substances they modify. So, for example, the formal reality possessed by one of his ideas, he said, was derived from the formal reality possessed by his mind. (AT VII 41; CSM II 28). Clearly, in order for the mind to "give" some of its formal reality to one of its modes, it must possess enough to give, and yet in the end, in remaining a substance, still possess more than the mode. The level of formal reality possessed by finite substances, then, is greater than that possessed by modes. But the buck doesn't stop with finite substances. The level of formal reality possessed by an infinite substance, Descartes insisted, is greater than the level of formal reality possessed by a finite substance. Perhaps like the case of the mode, a finite substance can be said to derive its formal reality from that of the infinite substance. Therefore, we can say that Descartes took there to be at least three levels of actual (formal) being in the cosmos:

> **Infinite Substance**
> **Finite Substance**
> **Mode**

He took God to be the infinite substance; mind and body to be finite substances; he took ideas, judgments, and desires, to be instances of modes of mind; and he took sizes, shapes, and motions to be instances of modes of body. As noted earlier, these ontological items are asymmetrically related. A mode is less real than a finite substance insofar as a mode depends for its existence on the existence of a finite substance in a way that a finite substance does not depend for its existence on any of its modes. Likewise, a finite substance is less real than an infinite substance insofar as a finite substance depends for its existence on the existence of an infinite substance in a way that an infinite substance does not depend for its existence on a finite substance. The relation is transitive, of course, and so a mode ultimately will depend for its existence on the existence of an infinite substance. In fact, according to Descartes's ontology, *all* finite beings depend for their existence on the existence of the infinite being–it should be clear by now that Descartes took this infinite being to be what theologians denoted by the word "God."

Metaphysical Rock Bottom

Since all things depend (ontologically) on God, and God doesn't depend (ontologically) on anything, the absolute ontological rock bottom of the cosmos is God. That was Descartes's view. Nevertheless, he adopted versions of two classic "proofs" for God's existence–versions of the ontological and cosmological arguments–which could give the impression that he thought God's existence was debatable. But, it was only so, he thought, if one was confused about what God was. The "proofs" were intended for his readers. They were part of the philosophical method he employed to help readers "clean" their otherwise murky minds, clouded by sensory experience and beliefs adopted during their upbringing and education. The aim was to help a reader become *clear and distinct*—as opposed to being *obscure and confused*—the latter, he thought, being the typical reader's mental state.

Getting clear and distinct, as we might call it, involves a proper organizing of our ideas. Sometimes Descartes said that his aim was to help his readers form clear and distinct ideas. In other places, he stated that the aim was to help them remove whatever obscures or confuses their ideas, which, once removed, would reveal the clear and distinct (the *un*obscured and *un*confused) ideas underneath. To say that you are clear and distinct, then, is to say that your ideas are properly organized, no longer obscuring one another or confused (literally "mixed together") with one another.

The "proofs" for God's existence were needed, as just noted, since many of Descartes's readers didn't have a clear and distinct idea of God—instead, they had adhered to the Catholic Church's portrayal of a really big, powerful, bearded guy in a robe, sitting on a throne somewhere in heaven. This idea is obscure and confused for lots of reasons, the least of which is its depiction of God as corporeal—that is, as having a body, as having a spatial location, and so on. The idea of body, in this case, is *mixed with* the idea of God (so, the idea is *confused*). So the existence of that really big bearded guy can easily be doubted. But, as just noted, once clear and distinct, the idea of God would compel us to affirm His existence. Again, keep in mind that saying you are clear and distinct (with respect to the idea of God) is just another way of declaring that your idea of God is clear and distinct.

This idea would also exhibit God's existence as being simply coextensive with God's being. They are one and the same thing. Using Descartes's lingo, when clear and distinct, you'd understand that God's *existence* and God's *being* are only conceptually distinct. Although we needn't go into the proofs he employed, it will be helpful to consider the one that turns on the concept of *formal reality*, since that's the concept now being discussed. So, let's do that briefly before bringing this chapter to a close.

In the Third Meditation, Descartes presented the view that every effect must have a cause, where the "reality" of the effect comes from (is derived from) or is traced back to the "reality" of the cause. It's a pretty simple view. Let's say that we come across a pot of water and notice that it's really hot. Water's not normally hot, so we figure that something must be the source of the heat. We then notice that this pot is hanging just above a small fire. Let's agree that we're convinced this fire is the source of the water's heat. The heat in the water is the effect of the influence of the fire. Conversely, the fire is the cause of the heat we detect in the water. Now, according to Descartes, there must be as much heat in the fire as there is heat in the water. For, if this wasn't the case, some of the heat of the water would've come from nothing, and that's not possible! This holds not only for water and heat and what not, but for everything. Descartes wrote:

> A stone, for example, which previously did not exist, cannot begin to exist unless it is produced by something which contains, either formally or eminently everything to be found in the stone; similarly, heat cannot be produced in an object which was not previously hot, except by something of at least the same order <or degree or kind> of perfection as heat, and so on. But it is also true that the *idea* of heat, or of a stone, cannot exist in me unless it is put there by some cause which contains at least as much reality as I conceive to be in the heat or in the stone. (Third Meditation, AT VII 41; CSM II 28)

This had some impact on Descartes's examination of his idea of God, which, as you remember, is the idea of an infinite being. As he told us in the passage just quoted, the contents of all of his ideas must have a cause. And, since the idea of God represents an *infinite* being, this idea (its representational content) must be caused by something that has at least as much reality as is found represented to him in his idea. For what holds for formal reality also holds for another kind of reality, which Descartes called *objective reality*. As we'll discuss further in the next chapter, Descartes noted that objective reality is the kind of reality that our ideas possess in virtue of their representing things to us. The basic notion is this:

Objective Reality is the kind of reality an idea possesses insofar as it represents something.

An idea will possess both kinds of reality. Insofar as it is an actual (existent), occurring mode of a mind, it possesses formal reality, and insofar as it represents something it possesses objective reality. And although objective reality cannot exist independent of a mind (unlike formal reality), since it is something it requires a cause. (AT VII 41; CSM II 28-29)

Ultimately, Descartes said, objective reality must have its origin in or must be traceable to, a thing that possesses formal reality. (AT VII 42; CSM II 29) As he put it:

The nature of an idea is such that of itself it requires no formal reality except what it derives from my thought, of which it is a mode. But in order for a given idea to contain such and such objective reality, it must surely derive it from some cause which contains at least as much formal reality as there is objective reality in the idea. (AT VII 41; CSM II 28)

So, here's the gist of the proof: my idea of God represents God as being infinite. This is to say that the "level" of objective reality possessed by the idea is greater than that which represents to me a finite substance or a mode. Since whatever caused this level of objective reality must possess at least as much formal reality as that level of objective reality possessed by the idea, it follows that whatever caused this idea (its representational content) must have a level of formal reality that is greater than that possessed by a finite substance. This greater level is that associated with an infinite substance. Now, my (existent) mind is simply finite, and so it possesses the level of formal reality of that of a finite substance. So, my mind cānnot be the cause of my idea of God (it cannot be the cause of its content). Instead, its cause must be a being that possesses a level of formal reality associated with being an infinite substance. Since when saying that a thing possesses formal reality is basically the same as saying that this thing exists, then this infinite substance exists. And, Descartes stated, this infinite being is what people normally refer to by the name "God." Therefore, God exists.

Now, how might this help us better understand the dependence relation? We can answer this by first noting that Descartes also seemed to have adopted the theological doctrine that God is a *unity*, and is not "divisible" in any way. If we say that God wills or that God understands, even though *we* take the willing and the understanding to be distinct "actions," the fact of the matter is that they are not distinct–at least they are not modally or really distinct. The distinction is, again, only conceptual. This opens the door to an argument that helps to make some sense of the above connection between *formal reality* and being *actual*. It was earlier noted that for Descartes formal reality was taken to be the kind of reality a thing possessed insofar as it was an actual thing. The Sun was an example of something that possesses formal reality, while Pegasus was an example of something that does not possess it. This formal-reality speak, it was suggested, could substitute for our saying things like "The Sun *exists*" and "Pegasus does *not* exist." That is, saying that a thing possesses formal reality could be construed as a way of saying that this thing *exists*. We know that in Descartes's view all finite substances–mind and body–derive their formal reality from God, the infinite substance. This is a sense in which God ontologically underwrites the existence of finite mind and body. Conversely, this is a sense in which finite mind and body depend for their existence on God.

So, consider again that with respect to God the various "actions" that we attribute to God, such as willing, judging, understanding, thinking, creating, and the like, are only *conceptually* distinct from one another. Thus, there is no real distinction between God's thinking about the Sun, say, and God's willing the Sun, or God's creating the Sun, and so on. And in God's doing any of these things, the Sun is, consequently, an *actual* being—that is, the Sun, in being something that God thinks (wills, creates, etc.), is real or possesses formal reality—in short, it is something that *exists*. As we noted earlier, however, it's not clear whether Descartes would take *the Sun* to be itself a substance, or something that God cognizes. Rather, he seemed to have thought that *body* (or *res extensa*, the *extended thing*, as he sometimes called it) is the substance that God thinks, and the Sun is nothing more than some "carved out" region of body—a region of the *extended thing*—the "carving out" done by way of motions introduced by God, which, in turn, serve to determine an inscribed region's shape and size. So, the view is better put by saying that body, a finite substance, is *real* or *actualized* by way of God's thinking (willing, creating, etc.) it.

You can see that things are different with respect to your mind. Just because you think of something, it won't follow that that thing exists. Pegasus is a good example. So, human (finite) minds are not like God's in *every* way (though Descartes did say that they are like God's mind in important ways (AT VII 57; CSM II 40)). What would happen if God thought about Pegasus? Presumably, Pegasus would be as real as the Sun. Human minds think the Sun and Pegasus; God doesn't think about such things—in the case of material reality, God simply thinks *body*, into which motion is introduced. The introduction of motion, as suggested above, gives rise to modally distinct "carved up" regions of the one huge though finite extension (where to one of those regions human minds have given the name "the Sun"). That said, we will continue to work with the example of the Sun, where it is helpful to do so, since Descartes himself liked to employ it on occasion. The point to stress here, then, is that a finite substance exists, or possesses formal reality, insofar as God thinks it (wills it, creates it, etc.).

The chapters that follow will deal specifically with the ontological and epistemological items brought to light in this chapter. We'll first turn to examine Descartes's notion of mind. Then we'll look more carefully at his epistemology. After that, we'll turn to examine his notion of body, and to take a more careful look at his physics and his mechanization of "life." Ultimately, these chapters will allow us to examine his notion of the human being. By book's end, you should have a solid understanding of Descartes's philosophical view.

2. Mind

In Chapter 1, we learned that Descartes believed there were two kinds of things in the cosmos: *mind* and *body*. Each has a principal attribute that constitutes its essence or nature—that which accounts for its being the kind of thing it is. He took the principal attribute of body to be *extension* and the principal attribute of mind to be *thought* or *thinking*. Thinking is what makes a mind the kind of thing it is. This chapter will focus on Descartes's notion of mind.

So, what is *thinking*? What is it you are doing when you are *thinking*? That's a tough question. You'd think (no pun intended) that thinking would be easy to identify, since it is what you do whenever you do what you do. Perhaps we might begin an answer to this question by noting, as Descartes told us, that whatever the mind is, it isn't a body. A body is a completely different kind of thing. Since a body is essentially extended, then if a mind isn't a body, we at least can know that it isn't extended. Okay, so the mind is essentially a thing that thinks. So, what is that? Descartes answered: "A thing that doubts, understands, affirms, denies, is willing, is unwilling, and also imagines and has sensory perceptions." (Second Meditation, AT VII 28; CSM II 19) All of those "activities"—doubting, understanding, judging, imagining, sensing, and so on—are instances of thinking.

In the previous chapter, we briefly considered Dutch philosopher Baruch Spinoza's take on Descartes. Considering the interpretations of other philosophers of the same era can be useful when trying to get a better understanding of his view. This being the case, let's consider another 17th-century philosopher who had adopted a version of Descartes's view: the French priest, Nicolas Malebranche (1638-1750). In his book, *The Search After Truth* (c. 1674), Malebranche accepted the fact that we have no satisfactory idea of the mind, no idea that makes clear to us what a mind is or what thinking is. That would certainly explain why we're at a loss to say what thinking is. Even so, he recognized that some things could be said about mind and its activity.

Descartes had suggested that the mind has two basic *faculties* or *capacities*. The first is what he called the *intellect* or the *understanding*, and the second is what he referred to as the *will*. In addition to these two basic faculties, he recognized several others—for instance, the faculties of memory, imagination, and sensory perception. These were not *basic*, since in order to "activate" them the mind would have to be "embodied." That is, it would have to be put in a special relation to body, something that Descartes thought God does when creating human beings. We'll take a look at Descartes's view of this *union* in Chapter 6. So, more on that later. Now let's get back to mind and see if we can use Malebranche's ideas to make some of this clearer.

In the *Search* (Book One, Chapter One), he focused on the two basic faculties: the *understanding* and the *will*. The first faculty, the understanding, is the capacity that the mind possesses, which allows it to have *ideas*. We'll take a closer look at ideas shortly; suffice it to say for now that the understanding (or better, an *idea* occurring in the understanding) accounts for the *what* of thinking. For instance, if you are thinking about pizza, the *what* of thinking is the thing you're thinking about—the pizza. It's the object of your thinking. In Descartes's lingo, we'd say that you are having the *idea* of pizza, or perhaps more specifically, the idea that *represents* pizza to you (obviously, we are using pizza as an example to illustrate this point; Descartes would not have known what pizza is.) This idea would be a mode of thought or thinking that is representing a pizza *to you*, where *you* are the perceiving subject. The understanding, then, is your mind's capacity to represent things to you.

The faculty of the will is the capacity of the mind that allows it to *incline* toward some good. It is *you* who is being inclined. So, the faculty of the will, as Malebranche put it, is that from which an *impulse* originates in a mind, the impulse that directs you (your mind) toward some good. That sounds weird, but there are ways of dispelling some of the weirdness. Malebranche said that the faculty of the will is "[the] capacity the soul has of loving different goods, *the impression or natural impulse that carries us toward general and indeterminate good."* (*Search*, Book One, Chapter One, p. 5) Now, since the mind also has the faculty of the understanding, it will have ideas. Malebranche disagreed with Descartes on "where" ideas were ultimately "located." Descartes thought that the ideas are modifications of *your* mind; whereas Malebranche believed they didn't belong to your mind but to God's. Be that as it may, they both seemed to have thought that ideas can "direct" the impulse, the one originating in the faculty of the will, specifically toward themselves. So, instead of your volitional (willful) impulse being directed at good *in general* or at *indeterminate* good, given the presence of an idea in the understanding, it will now be directed at a particular good, like the pizza that is represented to you by way of the idea. So, the basic "structure" of the mind, in this view, is that an idea arises by way of the faculty of the understanding, an idea that represents a particular thing (that is, a particular "good"), while simultaneously an impulse arises from or by way of the faculty of the will, which is directed at the particular thing represented.

Notice that the directedness of the volitional impulse is *one way*: it arises from the faculty of will and is directed at the faculty of the understanding. It's worth noting that since the mind isn't extended, *directedness*, especially if we're talking about the will being *directed at* an idea, as though the faculty of the will was "located" here and the faculty of the understanding was "located" there, is metaphorical—instructive but metaphorical. Philosophers that followed in the wake of Descartes and Malebranche, like Immanuel Kant, Johann Gottlieb Fichte, Franz Brentano, Edmund Husserl, and others, would interpret this view as telling us that insofar as the mind sports this inherent *directedness*, which they called *intentionality*, the relationship that holds between the *subject* of experience (the "I" of experience) and the *object* of experience (the idea) is essential for any state of *consciousness*. The *subject* is associated here with the faculty of the will, the *object* with the faculty of the understanding. We might picture it this way:

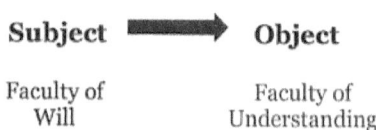

Faculty of Will   Faculty of Understanding

In the Third Meditation, Descartes worked out something like this basic picture, though admittedly it is a bit murky. Having posited the two basic faculties, he turned to further analyzing thinking, or thought, and wrote:

> Some of my thoughts are as it were the images of things, and it is only in these cases that the term "idea" is strictly appropriate—for example, when I think of a man, or a chimera, or the sky, or an angel, or God. Other thoughts have various additional forms: thus when I will, or am afraid, or affirm, or deny, there is always a particular thing which I take as the object of my thought, but my thought includes something more than the likeness of that thing. Some thoughts in this category are called volitions or emotions, while others are called judgments. (AT VII 37; CSM II 25-26)

In the Fourth Meditation, where he emphasized the will and the understanding, he said that affirming, which is a species of *judging*, is the will's assenting to (the truth of) an idea. We'll say more about this in the next chapter. For now, suffice it to say that some ideas compel the assent of the will, and some don't. But that doesn't stop a naïve mind from assenting anyway. It's in the latter sorts of cases,

Descartes noted, that the possibility of error in judgment arises. More on that later.

We can take what he wrote in the Fourth Meditation and make better sense of what he had said (quoted above) in the Third Meditation. Here's one way to understand Descartes's view: let's say that you have the idea of the Pythagorean Theorem, which describes the relationship between the sides of a Euclidean right triangle. Not only are you *aware of* this theorem, which requires that your mind be "directed" at it in some sense, but in this case, you also judge it to be true. So, you consider this idea, and are compelled to think that it (what it represents) is true—your will, in other words, has been compelled to assent. Using Malebranche's expression, we account for the presence of the idea by appealing to the faculty of the understanding, and we account for the origin of the inclination to "assent" by appealing to the faculty of the will.

In light of our picture of the structure of the mind, and taking seriously certain suggestions offered by philosophers like Kant and Husserl, it is probably not far off course to suggest, as suggested above, that in your *being aware of* some object (represented by way of an idea) the will is in play, since your being aware can be cast as the directedness originating in the faculty of the will. In holding that a mind is always *conscious* or *aware of* something, both faculties must be taken to always be in play. The mind isn't static; it's never in a state when only one of the two basic faculties is working. It *receives* representations, but in one's being *aware of* those representations, the mind is "active" with respect to them, it is directed at them. Moreover, as one's ideas change (as the representations change), there is also a kind of "movement" of a mind—its awareness "moving" from one object to another. Again, dynamic, not static.

Ideas

As we know, Descartes said that ideas are modes of the mind. In the "Preface to the Reader" of the *Meditations*, which looks to have been written after the *Meditations*, he took the opportunity to make things a bit clearer. He explained that the word "idea" is ambiguous:

> "Idea" can be taken materially, as an operation of the intellect, in which case it cannot be said to be more perfect than me. Alternatively, it can be taken objectively, as the thing represented by that operation; and this thing, even if it is not regarded as existing outside the intellect, can still, in virtue of its essence, be more perfect than myself. (AT VII 8; CSM II 7)

According to some scholars, the distinction that Descartes was drawing here is between considering an idea as an *act* of representation versus considering this same idea as the result of this act, as the *object* presented immediately to you. Some refer to this object as the idea's *content*.

Consider the sensory idea of the Sun which, taken *materially*, is the idea understood as an *act* of representation. It is whatever the mind is doing when it works at representing or at exhibiting something. On the other hand, the idea of the Sun taken *objectively* is the idea now understood as the *object exhibited* by way of this act—which is the Sun *as represented*. Now, according to the passage quoted above, the Sun as represented doesn't seem to be the Sun itself, that is, it doesn't seem to be the Sun in the sky. Such objects, as he said in the above passage, are not regarded as existing independently of the mind (i.e., outside the intellect). The objective-Sun, we might call it, the *object* exhibited directly to the mind by way of one of its acts, is a *mental* entity, something that depends on the mind, at least in part, for its existence. That said, Descartes did respond to a critic, Caterus, that "...the idea of the sun is the sun *itself* existing in the intellect—not of course formally existing, as it does in the heavens, but objectively existing, i.e., in the way in which objects normally are in the intellect." (First Set of Replies, AT VII 102; CSM II 75, emphasis mine) So here, he suggested that the Sun exhibited by way of the act of representing, the objective-Sun as it was just called, *is* the Sun, but existing in the mind and not independently of the mind (for Descartes, the "mental" Sun, the *object* exhibited by way of the idea, didn't possess formal reality).

In the Third Meditation, Descartes introduced another distinction, the one between formal and objective reality, which we considered earlier. Although some scholars think that this distinction is really no different from the one he later introduced in the "Preface to the Reader"–the distinction between taking an idea either materially or objectively–there are some differences between them worth noting. For instance, the material/objective distinction introduced in the "Preface," focuses on the relationship between an idea understood as an *act* of representation, and the very same idea understood as the *object represented* or *object exhibited* by way of this act. It focuses on the relationship between the act that produces an idea's content and the content produced. By contrast, the formal/objective reality distinction, also introduced in the Third Meditation, focuses on two relationships, namely the relationship between an idea understood as a mode of the mind, and the relationship between the idea's content and some other thing which, when not the mind, will be a thing possessing formal reality, a thing, in other words, that exists independently of the mind.

Think again about the idea of the Sun. Understood as a mode, we consider the idea's ontological status, which in this case means considering the formal reality it possesses. As we know from a passage quoted in Chapter 1, Descartes posited that the formal reality of an idea is derived from the formal reality of the mind, of which the idea is a mode. But what about the idea's objective reality? To answer this, first recall Descartes's position that the idea's objective reality is the kind of reality it possesses in virtue of its representing something. Here, we're talking about the idea's *content*–the *object exhibited*. What is the origin of the idea's objective reality? Descartes concluded that the objective reality of the idea of the Sun has its origin in the formal reality of the Sun. That is, the object exhibited (in the idea) has its origin in the Sun that exists independently of the mind. This, in fact, will be the sense in which the idea is said to represent *the Sun* and not some other object.

The following analogy may be helpful. Suppose that Descartes was standing in front of a mirror. There are at least two things in the room: Descartes and the mirror. Since both are "real" things, both possess some level of formal reality. On the mirror's surface, we see an *image* of Descartes. The image is *of* him in the sense that it represents him. Notice that we don't say that the image represents the mirror, even though it is "located" on the mirror. This image, the image of Descartes, requires both the existence of Descartes and the mirror. If we destroyed either, the image of Descartes would be destroyed. Notice, also, that if we destroyed the image of Descartes by destroying the mirror, we would do nothing to Descartes. This is because the image of Descartes depends for its existence (and being) on the existence of Descartes, but he does not depend for his existence (or being) on the existence of this image (or the mirror). Clearly, then, there is an important relation holding between the mirror and this image, since the mirror is in part causally responsible for producing the image. And, there is an equally important relationship between Descartes and this image, since Descartes is in part causally responsible for producing the image. So, both the mirror and Descartes play causal roles in producing the image.

But Descartes and the mirror must be playing importantly *distinct* causal roles, since we say that the image is *of* Descartes—that is, the image represents *Descartes*. Putting this in Descartes's terms, the mirror's image, as an image "located" on the mirror's surface, is a mode of the mirror. It is a way in which the mirror is being modified. Insofar as any such image exists, it derives its existence from the mirror. This is akin to saying that the formal reality possessed by the image, understood as a mode of the mirror, is derived from the formal reality of the substance it modifies, the mirror. But when considering the *content* of the image, what it represents or exhibits, we must appeal to something other than the mirror. We must appeal to Descartes. Again, using Descartes's explanation, we might say that taking the image understood in terms of its content is to take the image objectively—that is, in terms of the objective reality it possesses. According to a passage quoted earlier, we might say that the origin of this objective reality is the formal reality possessed by Descartes. In other words, the content of the image has its origin in the thing, the *existing* thing, standing in front of the mirror. (You can't have mirror images of non-existent things; so given that Descartes no longer exists, there can no longer be any mirror images of him.) So, we say that the image represents Descartes because the objective reality possessed by the image (the kind of reality in terms of which it represents) has its origin in the formal reality of Descartes.

A similar analysis of ideas can be made. Descartes took the paradigm example of an idea to be the idea of God. Insofar as the idea is a mode of Descartes's mind, he can account for the formal reality it possesses (in terms of which it is said to be a "real" or "existent" mode). Its formal reality is derived from the formal reality of his own mind. The challenge, as set out in the Third Meditation, is his accounting for the objective reality possessed by the idea. Since the idea represents or presents to him an infinite being, the level of objective reality is greater than that possessed by an idea that represents or presents a finite thing. As we learned in the previous chapter, Descartes concluded that the cause of this idea—that is, the cause of its content—must possess a level of formal reality great enough to account for the level of objective reality possessed by the idea. Since the level of formal reality possessed by his own mind is not great enough, he noted that he, or his mind, cannot be its origin. Rather, its origin must be a thing possessing the level of formal reality associated with an infinite being, which, as we now know, is God. In fact, this is the sense in which Descartes's idea is *of* God.

The same, it seems, would hold for the idea of the Sun. Insofar as it is a mode of his mind, the idea has its origin in his mind, of which it is a mode. The formal reality possessed by the idea, in other words, is derived from the formal reality of his mind. But the objective reality of the sensory idea of the Sun has a different origin. It has its origin in the formal reality of the Sun. This is the sense in which the idea is *of* the Sun. Now, as was also noted earlier, it's not clear whether Descartes would take the Sun to be a thing, a substance, distinct from, say, the Moon. It may have been his view that there was only one *body*, the *extended thing*, where the Sun and the Moon were nothing more than modally distinct regions of the one extended substance. In the Sixth Meditation, he did argue that the objective reality of his idea of body must have its origin in an actually existing body, in an existing corporeal substance. (AT VII 79f; CSM II 55f) This, of course, means that body, insofar as it is "real," possesses some level of formal reality. But whether his talk of *body* here includes things like the Sun and Moon, or just the one extended thing, is up in the air. So, it could have been Descartes's view that the ideas of the Sun and Moon were, after philosophical analysis, to be understood as ideas of body.

The point here is that when applying the formal/objective reality distinction to ideas, the result focuses on *two* relationships: the first is the relationship idea *as mode* has to the mind; the second is the relationship idea *as content* or *as object exhibited* has to what the idea represents or is *of*. This seems to be importantly different from the material/objective distinction. For, when this latter distinction is applied to ideas, the result focuses on *one* relationship: the relationship between the idea *as act* and the idea (this very same idea) *as content produced* by way of this act. So, although it may be true that the terms *material* and *formal* are related (maybe even synonymous), and the terms *objective* in both distinctions are related (maybe even identical), the distinctions themselves—*formal/objective reality distinction* and *material/objective distinction*—are importantly different, and are not simply two ways of expressing the same distinction.

Innate, Adventitious, and Factitious Ideas

In the Third Meditation, Descartes recognized three different kinds of idea: *innate, adventitious,* and *factitious*. His first examples of innate ideas are those whose contents he accounted for by simply appealing to his own nature. So, the idea of thinking, or of what thought is, can be accounted for by appealing to the fact that he is a mind, which is a thing that essentially thinks. The idea's objective reality, which accounts for the idea's representing what it does, can be understood as originating in the formal reality of his own mind. Adventitious ideas, he said, are those whose contents do more than suggest that their objective reality has its origin in things existing "outside" his mind—that is, originating in things that exist independently of his mind. So, for example, the adventitious idea of the Sun (i.e., the *sensory* idea of the Sun) does more than to suggest that it has its origin in the Sun. That is, this idea leads him to think that the idea is of the Sun because the idea's objective reality has its origin in the formal reality of the Sun. Factitious ideas, he wrote, are those whose contents come from the contents of other ideas. Therefore, he can account for their objective reality by an appeal to the objective reality of some other idea. Pegasus is a good example of a factitious idea. One simply takes from the ideas of a horse, a bird, and so on, and fabricates the idea of a winged horse. (Whenever Descartes talked about *chimeras*, he meant fictional objects like Pegasus.)

There are troubles lurking here if we don't clean some of this up. In addition to his innate idea of a mind, Descartes included at least two other ideas in the innate category: the idea of God and the idea of body—despite the fact that he couldn't account for their contents by an appeal to his own mind. Instead, his arguments turned to showing that the content (the objective reality) of the idea of God has its origin in the formal reality of God (Third Meditation, AT VII 45*f*; CSM II 31*f*); and the content (the objective being) of the idea of body has its origin in the formal reality of body (Sixth Meditation, AT

VII 79f; CSM II 54f). Since both God and body are cast as possessing formal reality, it follows that both *exist* independently of Descartes's mind. Because of this, those two innate ideas, the ideas of God and body, look better cast as adventitious. This is the trouble that seems to be lurking. Let's see if we can't clean things up so that we might set aside this potential glitch.

In the *Principles of Philosophy*, Descartes wrote that the ideas of infinite mind (God), finite mind, and finite (indefinite) body, are the principles of philosophy. What he likely meant by this is that he could account for everything in his system in terms of these three ideas. In a letter to Princess Elisabeth of Bohemia, with whom he corresponded over the years, Descartes referred to his innate ideas as *primitive notions*. He noted that they are "as it were the patterns on the basis of which we form all our other conceptions." (AT III 665; CSMK III 218) In a later letter, he included a fourth idea, that of the *union* of mind and body. (AT III 691; CSMK III 226) In both letters, he made it clear that these ideas stand on their own. We cannot derive one from the other. So, perhaps the view isn't that they are innate because he could account for the origin of their contents by appealing to his mind, or to his own nature—as he had said in the Third Meditation—but are innate in the sense that they are *presupposed* in anything we may think. As he wrote in the earlier letter just quoted, these ideas serve as the patterns that *inform* our thinking. Anything we may think about presupposes at least one of these more primitive ideas, which, interestingly, may be what in the Third Meditation he called *primary ideas*.

About the latter he said:

> For just as the objective mode of being belongs to ideas by their very nature, so the formal mode of being belongs to the causes of ideas—or at least the first and most important ones—by *their* very nature. And although one idea may perhaps originate from another, there cannot be an infinite regress here; eventually one must reach a primary idea, the cause of which will be like an archetype which contains

formally <and in fact> all the reality <or perfection> which is present only objectively <or representatively> in the idea. (AT VII 41-42; CSM II 29)

The innate ideas of God, mind, and body (and maybe even union) meet the criterion as set out in this passage. They are ideas whose objective reality has its origin in the formal reality of these "archetypal" items—infinite thinking substance, finite thinking substance, and finite (indefinite) body—the items serving as the patterns for all other ideas.

Freedom, Error, and the Will

In the Fourth Meditation, Descartes worked out an account of the possibility of error in judgment, which suggested an account of freedom. Let's briefly look at each before bringing this chapter to a close. We'll look more closely at Descartes's view on freedom and how it connects to his view of moral action in Chapter 6, which focuses on his perspective on the human being. But since *judging* is an act of the mind, a better grasp of this notion, as well as the error that can be made in this context, will help us understand Descartes's notion of mind.

Recall the two basic faculties: the understanding and the will. The *human* mind, Descartes said, is finite. One sense in which it is finite is in respect to the faculty of the understanding. The human mind only knows, and can only know, so much at any given time. Although it may increase its knowledge over time, it will never reach the place where it is omniscient, or all-knowing. As noted in the previous sections, some of our ideas compel the assent of the will. This is another way of saying that we *affirm* their truth. To affirm is *to judge*. Such ideas are said to be clear and distinct. We'll say more about this in the next chapter. Now, in contrast to those ideas that compel assent, some of our ideas don't compel the assent of the will. The will is left unaffected, at least when it comes to judgment (that the will is "directed" at the idea shows that the will is "doing" something even pre-judgment). Assenting, or judging, is the willful act of asserting that something is *true*; in this case, the truth of that which is exhibited by the idea. Of course, the will *can* assent anytime, but it isn't always being compelled to assent. When an idea doesn't compel assent, it is said to be either obscure or confused, or both obscure and confused. To be sure, if you assent to such an idea you may get lucky, where the idea may turn out to be true after all. But here you'd only be lucky. Your assent wasn't based on any sign or indication of truth. And in being lucky, no one would count this as your having knowledge. But let's say that this idea was false, and yet you assented. Clearly, you'd be making a *false* judgment, or as Descartes put it, you'd be making an error in judgment. You've misused the faculty of judgment (the will). So, error in judgment is *possible* whenever you assent to an idea that is in the group of ideas that don't compel assent. "[T]he scope of the will," Descartes said, "is wider than that of the intellect; but instead of restricting it within the same limits, I extend its use to matters which I do not understand." (AT VII 58; CSM II 40) You'd be guaranteed the truth, Descartes posited, if you limited your assent to those ideas that compel assent. But when you extend assent to ideas that don't compel assent, supposing that you lack any reason for assenting, you run the risk of error in judgment.

Freedom, according to Descartes, is the assent of the will to a good that is clearly and distinctly exhibited by an idea. It is when one is compelled to assent that one is "wholly free." (AT VII 58; CSM II 40) When not compelled, one is in a state of indifference, and in such a state one is less free than when in a state of being compelled. He said:

> But the indifference I feel when there is no reason pushing me in one direction rather than another is the lowest grade of freedom; it is evidence not of any perfection of freedom, but rather of a defect in knowledge or a kind of negation. For

if I always saw clearly what was true and good, I should never have to deliberate about the right judgement or choice; in that case, although I should be wholly free, it would be impossible for me ever to be in a state of indifference. (AT VII 58; CSM II 40)

To say that one is most free when one is compelled sounds contradictory. It would seem that if one is *compelled*, one isn't free at all. But Descartes said that it is when we're compelled that we're most free. And, it is when we are indifferent, not compelled this way or that, that we are less free. But you'd think that if one is indifferent, one would be *most* free. Let's straighten this out.

Descartes clearly disagreed with the sort of analysis just offered. Remember that a clear and distinct idea is one that compels the assent of the will. In Descartes's view, the relation between truth, goodness, and the compulsion of the will, has been divinely instituted. Let's say that you are presented with two courses of action. Descartes noted:

> In order to be free, there is no need for me to be inclined both ways; on the contrary, the more I incline in one direction—either because I clearly understand that reasons of truth and goodness point that way, or because of a divinely produced disposition of my inmost thoughts—the freer is my choice. (AT VII 57-58; CSM II 40)

Suppose, then, that there are two apples put before you—one safe to eat and the other not safe, for it has been poisoned. The safe apple is green, the deadly apple is red. Now, let's say that you have not eaten for a long time and need to eat something soon or risk death. The apples are the only things available to eat at this particular moment. So, assuming that you have chosen to continue to live, you've got a choice: eat the green or the red apple (or both). Since you understand that the poisoned apple will kill you, and death is what you want to avoid, choosing the green apple is the only choice. To be sure, you're "free" to choose either, but given your aim (to continue to live), the choice is clear. Knowing that the green apple is safe to eat allows you to fulfill your aim to continue to live. This knowledge certainly narrowed things down to one choice, but this choice is precisely the one that allows you to fulfill your goal. This is what makes it the *right* choice.

Contrast that with not knowing which apple was poisoned. You're starving. Which apple do you choose? Here, you'd be in a state of limbo, or as Descartes put it, you'd be indifferent. You wouldn't know which apple to choose. That, Descartes said, doesn't look as good as the previous scenario in which you knew which apple was safe to eat. The second scenario, the one in which you are at a loss as to which apple to choose, is a *lesser* kind of freedom in an important sense. Being in a state of ignorance or indifference prohibits you from pursuing your aims, which is more of an obstruction than anything. Thus, when the will is *compelled* in one direction over another, which implies that truth and goodness has been exhibited to you, you are in fact *most* free, since you are now in a position to pursue and fulfill your aims. The compelling of the will, in this case, is simply another way of saying that you now *know* which choice is best. Descartes took that to be *freedom* in the strongest sense possible.

3. The Search for Truth and Certainty

In this chapter, we will look more carefully at Descartes's notions of *truth*, *certainty*, *clarity* and *distinctness* (and the latter's counterparts, *obscurity* and *confusion*), as well as the compelling of the will.

The theory of truth that Descartes very likely inherited from his teachers was an Aristotelian *correspondence* theory of truth. We considered a version of this theory in Chapter 1. The basics of the theory tell us that *truth* arises as a certain relation holding between a proposition (or declarative sentence) and a fact. As was noted, the proposition is a linguistic entity; the fact is an ontological entity, a constituent of reality. When a proposition picks out a fact in all the right ways—that is, the proposition *corresponds* to a fact—the proposition is said to be *true*. In some of Descartes's work, he seemed to have something like this in mind. But scholars find an alternate theory lurking about in the texts, which is based on Descartes's talk of *natures*. These, as we'll see, are not only the elements that constitute the essences of things, but also the inhabitants of the mind—they constitute the contents of our ideas. So, it looks like they play dual roles. Truth in this view is not something attributed to *propositions*, but to ideas, and in particular to the contents of our ideas. Talk of *truth* is related to those natures exhibited to us in or by way of our ideas.

Truth and Being

In Descartes's view, when you clearly and distinctly perceive something, you are presented with something that is *true*. He also said that when we are aware of something that is true, we are aware of something that is *real*. "It is obvious," he wrote, "that whatever is true is something." (Fifth Meditation, AT VII 65; CSM II 45) As noted in Chapter 1, by "real" in this context Descartes meant that this something exists independently of his (or any finite) mind. Using Descartes's more technical lingo, as he put it in his reply to Caterus, a real or actual thing possesses formal reality; insofar as it does, if this thing isn't the mind itself (or one of its modes), it is something that exists independently of the mind. The upshot is that when clearly and distinctly perceiving something, one perceives something that is real, which, according to Descartes, is just another way of saying that one perceives something that is true.

This view looks like it might have its origin in the ancient Greek philosophers Parmenides and Plato, whose opinions were very different from the one that Aristotle would later hold. In short, Parmenides and Plato stated that there were two fundamental metaphysical categories: *Being* and *Non-Being*. Aligned with these were the epistemic categories of *Truth* and *Falsity*, and the moral categories of *Good* and *Evil*, respectively. In a letter to his friend and editor, Claude Clerselier, Descartes wrote that "Truth consists in *being*, and falsehood only in *non-being*." (AT V 356; CSMK III 377) Earlier in the letter, he said, "[T]here is no distinction between truth and the thing or substance that is true..." (AT V 355; CSMK III 377) And, later in the letter, which we'll discuss more fully in Chapter 6, he suggested that what is real is true, and these are coextensive with what is good. (AT V 357; CSMK III 378) Again, using Descartes's technical terminology: *true*, *real*, and *good* are only conceptually distinct.

Natures: Simple and Composite

In Chapter 1, we briefly considered what Descartes referred to as *simple natures*. He used this phrasing in a very early work, *Rules for* the *Direction of the Mind* (c. 1628). We learned that *extension* is a simple nature, *thinking* is a simple nature, *shape* and *size* are simple natures, as are *colors, smells, tastes,* and so on. At the very least, they inhabit our ideas, as when you have, say, the idea of body, or the idea of mind, or the idea of God, or the idea of a triangle, or the idea of the Sun, or the idea of Pegasus. Although talk of such natures has its place in the metaphysics, in the *Rules* Descartes focused on their epistemic relationships—which natures are known in terms of which others. Such natures are also part of our current topic—Descartes's epistemology.

In the Sixth Set of Replies, Descartes noted that there are two kinds of unity: *unity by nature* and *unity by composition.* (AT VII 423-424; CSM II 285-286) If analyzed properly, the idea of a body, he said, shows that its shape presupposes its being extended. In other words, the simple nature *shape* is shown to entail or to presuppose the simple nature *extension.* This is the sense in which something is a unity by nature. The idea of your doubting, for instance, shows that doubting presupposes thinking. So the simple nature *doubting* is shown to entail or to presuppose the simple nature *thinking.* Thus, the idea of a body and the idea of a mind, when properly analyzed, reveal things that are unities by nature.

Descartes considered someone who superficially reflects on his or her experience, where this person believes him or herself to be the very same thing that doubts and also walks (moves) from place to place. (AT VII 423-424; CSM II 285-286) What he or she fails to notice is that there is no entailment relation holding between *doubting,* say, and *motion.* Now, *doubting* entails *thinking,* not *extension;* and *motion* entails *extension,* not *thinking.* Descartes suggested that since no entailment relation is to be found in this person's experience (no connection between *thinking* and *being extended*), the nature of this person as exhibited in this idea is not a unity by nature. It is what he called a *unity by composition.* This *may* be a real thing, but Descartes's point was that since it is not revealed to be a unity by nature, it could easily turn out that this nature is not real in any sense that would allow it to exist independently of our idea. In any event, it would not be a nature about which we could have any knowledge, since nothing internal to the idea signifies its being unified (that is, no connection is seen).

The nature this person considers (namely, that he or she is a thing that both doubts and walks, say) could very well be something like the composite nature of Pegasus. As Descartes told Dutch theologian Frans Burman in an interview:

> Even though we can with the utmost clarity imagine the head of a lion joined to the body of a goat, or some such thing, it does not therefore follow that they exist, since we do not clearly perceive the link, so to speak, which joins the parts together. (AT V 160; CSMK III 343-344)

The nature of body is a unity by nature, as is the nature of mind. But the nature of a human being, as suggested by the above analysis, is not a unity by nature but is a unity by composition. For, the idea of the human being seems to have the same defect as the idea of the lion-headed goat has, namely, it lacks the requisite entailment relations that would reveal the unity of its parts. So, although human nature may be real, we nevertheless cannot know anything about how it is unified.

It will turn out that we have lots of ideas about both kinds of unities. As for unities by nature, we have our ideas of body and mind, but all our ideas of geometrical shapes are also examples of such natures. And since these natures *never* change and are *always* the same, Descartes said that they should be called "immutable and eternal." (AT VII 381; CSM II 262) Clearly, the adventitious (sensory) idea of the Sun would be like the above person's idea of him or herself thinking and walking about. The *shape* of the Sun, for instance, entails *extension* (not *thinking*), and the *heat* (the sensible quality) exhibited in the idea entails *thinking* (not *extension*). But neither *extension* nor *thinking* entail one another. The Sun, according to this analysis, is not a unity by nature, but is a unity by composition—at least if we're talking about the Sun that we sense. Contrast this with the astronomical idea of the Sun, which depicts an object that differs from the one we sense. This idea, for instance, exhibits the Sun as a spherically-shaped thing, in motion, much greater in size than the Earth, and so on. All other simple natures that don't entail *extension*, like *heat* and *color*, have been removed. Here, the remaining simple natures *shape*, *motion*, and *size* entail or presuppose the simple nature *extension*. Thusly conceived, this nature, which may be better understood simply as the nature of a *body*, is a unity by nature.

Unities by nature are real. By contrast, unities by composition may or may not be real. Since unities by nature are real, the simple natures that make them up are real too. What is interesting here is that even though a unity by composition may not be real, the simple natures that make it up are nevertheless real. Descartes suggested something like this in the First Meditation, when noting the difference between the things we may experience in dreams versus the things we sense when awake. He said that even though what we may dream about may not be real, the items the mind employs to fabricate those things (the "things" presented in the dream) must be real. (AT VII 20; CSM II 13-14) The items he specifically mentioned are *colors*, which we know from what he had said in the *Rules* are simple natures. Here, to use our new jargon, the things experienced in dreams may be unities by composition. And, for all we know, much of what we sense may be too. Be that as it may, it seems to be Descartes's view that all simple natures are real, regardless of whether they make up a unity by nature or a unity by composition. They are kind of like "atoms," where they serve as underlying conditions for our having any experience *of the world*. Given the connection between *real* and *true*, then, it follows that all ideas that exhibit unities by nature, insofar as they show things that are real, are true. The line of reasoning can go the other way, too—namely, given the connection between *real* and *true*, it follows that all ideas that are true exhibit things that are real.

Clarity and Distinctness

In Chapter 2, we mentioned *clarity* and *distinctness*. These were important notions for Descartes. Ideas that are clear and distinct, he said, are true. (Third Meditation, AT VII 35; CSM II 24) And we now know that in his view, whatever is true is something (real). So, clear and distinct ideas are ideas of real things (actual things, things that possess formal reality).

Descartes never really defined "clarity," at least not cleanly enough to avoid criticism. For example, in the *Principles*, he simply wrote that "I call a perception 'clear' when it is present and accessible to the attentive mind." (AT VIIIA 21; CSM I 207) In other places, he posited that clarity emerges when we have an immediate insight into a connection between the simple natures exhibited in an idea. (AT V 160; CSMK III 343-344) This connection cannot be contingent, but will be necessary. The *necessity* of the connection is understood, as noted above, in terms of entailment or presupposition (though, as we'll see shortly, the insight is best expressed by the latter). He again presented the example of the simple natures *shape* and *extension*: their connection is shown to be necessary insofar as we cannot conceive *shape* independently of *extension*. This is another way of saying that the simple nature *shape* presupposes *extension*. (Rules, AT X 421; CSM I 45-46, see also *Principles*, AT VIIIA 25; CSM I 210) We might take this to mean that the idea exhibiting the simple nature *shape* also shows the simple nature *extension*, whether we were initially aware of this necessity or not. But once we "see" this connection between them, the idea is said to be *clear* (or at least to be *clearer* than before). Whenever the necessary connection is absent, the idea is said to be *obscure*. The connection is either not there or is being "obscured" by some other elements (simple natures) that constitute the content of the idea. *Clarity* and *obscurity* are at opposite ends of the spectrum, so to speak. The clearer an idea, the less obscure it is; and the more obscure, the less clear.

An idea is *distinct*, Descartes wrote in the *Principles*, when what it exhibits is separated from all items (simple natures) that are not necessarily connected, where the idea exhibits *only* what is clear. (AT VIIIA 22; CSM I 207-208). This means that a distinct idea includes or shows only those simple natures that are necessarily related. If an idea includes or exhibits simple natures that are not necessarily related, the idea is said to be *confused*—it literally includes a *mixture* of unrelated simple natures—the Latin *confusio* means *mixed (fusio) with* or *together (con)*. Therefore, *distinctness* and *confusion* are opposites.

Consider the geometrical idea of a triangle. It is *clear* since the simple natures it exhibits, such as the simple natures *size* and *shape*, entail or presuppose the simple nature *extension*. And since this idea includes or exhibits only those simple natures that are necessarily related to the simple nature *extension*, the idea is *distinct*. Thus, the geometrical idea of a triangle is clear and distinct. Contrast this with the sensory idea of the Sun. The simple natures *heat* and *color* presuppose the simple nature *thinking* or *thought*; whereas the simple natures *size* and *shape* presuppose the simple nature *extension*. There is absolutely no conceivable connection between the simple nature *thinking* and the simple nature *extension*. (Recall that Descartes mentioned that their "unity," if we wanted to call it such, is merely a unity by composition. It is not the more robust unity by nature.) Consequently, this idea is *obscure*, at least to the degree that no connection between the simple natures *thinking* and *extension* is to be found. And, since the idea includes or exhibits simple natures that are not necessarily related, the idea is *confused*. Thus, the sensory idea of the Sun is obscure and confused.

Let's pause and make clearer the connection between Descartes's system of simple natures and his epistemology.

The System of Simple Natures

In the *Rules*, Descartes noted that the simple natures constitute a highly-ordered system. Remember that some simple natures, such as *size* and *shape*, entail or presuppose the simple nature *extension*, in the sense that the former are unintelligible when isolated from the latter. Another way to understand this is to see that whenever you are thinking of a shape, you are thinking of extension too. In fact, you could *never* think of a shape that was not extended.

You may have noticed that, according to Descartes's analysis, the simple natures center round two simple natures: *extension* and *thinking*. These, also recall, are what Descartes referred to as the two *principal attributes*. They constitute the essences or natures of the two kinds of thing that exist in the cosmos—*body* and *mind*. There are those simple natures that entail or presuppose *extension*, and those that entail or presuppose *thinking*. Descartes recognized several other attributes such as *existence*. But all simple natures involve or presuppose existence, so if we were trying to get a better sense of how the simple natures were ordered, an appeal to *existence* wouldn't help, since in terms of existence everything would be alike. (It's worth keeping in mind that to say that something is actual or exists is to say that it possesses formal reality.)

Descartes suggested that when two things are constituted of a similar simple nature, they share a *common nature*. He said that whenever things share a common nature, they can be understood as belonging to a *class*. (*Rules*, AT X 379f; CSM I 20f) This idea would serve as a path that allowed him to move back and forth from metaphysical considerations to epistemological ones. For example, insofar as the Sun and the Moon share the common nature *shape* (both are shaped), they can be understood as belonging to a class—the class of *shaped things*. Of course, we know that in Descartes's view, the simple nature *shape* presupposes *extension*. We also know that "The Sun is shaped" entails "The Sun is extended."

To say that "The Sun is shaped" assumes that "The Sun is extended," which is to say that in all conceivable cases where the first proposition is true, the second is true too. Up to this point, we have set *entailment* and *presupposition* side by side. Now is a good time to show how they are important concepts that are doing subtly different work.

Although we don't have the space to go too deeply into this, we can at least get some sense of the difference by noting that *entailment* will hold between propositions, whereas *presupposition* will hold between things (or between concepts of things), or in our case, between simple natures. So, as has been said several times already, the simple nature *shape* presupposes the simple nature *extension*. Here the point is that the very being or existence of the simple nature *shape* depends on the being and existence of the simple nature *extension*. Descartes took this to be coextensive with our saying that our *idea* of shape, that is, the idea that includes the simple nature *shape*, presupposes (includes in it) the simple nature *extension*. If we instead express this relation by way of proposition, as we just did in the case of the Sun, we say that the proposition "The Sun is shaped" entails the proposition "The Sun is extended." This, as also just mentioned, tells us that in every conceivable case in which the former proposition is true, the latter is true, too.

Putting Descartes's system in terms of classes can easily accommodate both the entailment and the presupposition relation. Here, we'd say that the class of *shaped-things* belongs to (or is included in) the class of *extended-things*. The inclusion of the class of shaped-things in the class of extended-things can accommodate Descartes's claim that the simple nature *shape* presupposes the simple nature *extension*. Anything that is shaped will be extended. The Sun is a member of the class of shaped-things, which can be expressed "The Sun is shaped." (Technically, we might say, "The Sun is a shaped-thing".) Since the class of shaped-things is included in the class of extended-things, the Sun will, in virtue of being included in the class of shaped-things, be included in the class of extended-things, which allows us then to say, "The Sun is extended."

The Search for Truth and Certainty | 49

This class-included-in-a-class structure also accommodates the entailment relation—in every case in which "The Sun is shaped" is true, "The Sun is extended" is true too. Even though there is a difference here, let's not worry too much about that, and continue to talk of both, since in the end, we can always move from presupposition-talk to entailment-talk, and vice versa.

There are two basic mutually exclusive classes in Descartes's system—the class of *extended-things* and the class of *thinking-things*. All things included in the former share the common nature *extension*; whereas all things included in the latter share the common nature *thinking*. Modes, such as *shape* and *doubting*, then, are subsets, or are included in, one of these two basic classes. For instance, as just noted, the class of *shaped-things* is included in the class of *extended-things*, whereas the class of *doubting-things* is included in the class of *thinking-things*. Since both *extension* and *thinking* entail or presuppose *existence*, the corresponding classes of *extended-things* and *thinking-things* are included in the class of *existing-things* (or things possessing formal reality).

Understanding the order of this system (Descartes called it an *enumeration*), we can now better grasp the notions of *clarity* and *distinctness*. If an idea exhibits the entailment (or presupposition) relation between the simple natures constituting the idea—so, for instance, the idea of body exhibits the entailment (or presupposition) relation between the simple natures *shape* and *extension*—the idea is *clear*. By contrast, if an idea fails to demonstrate this, then the idea is *obscure*. Some ideas, like the sensory idea of the Sun, will exhibit this relation with respect to some of the simple natures in the idea, but not with respect to all. Thus, this idea, though perhaps clear regarding some of its content (its shape presupposes its extension), will be obscure with respect to other parts of its content (its extension and its heat, the quality felt, are not internally related). Such ideas, then, can be said to be more or less clear (or more or less obscure). Innate ideas, Descartes insisted, are maximally clear. This sets them apart from our other ideas.

Now, if an idea includes *only* those simple natures that share a common nature (ultimately sharing either the common nature *extension* or *thinking*), the idea is *distinct*. By contrast, if an idea includes simple natures that share more than one common nature (more than one of the two principal attributes), the idea is *confused*. So, the idea of a triangle, say, is distinct in this sense, since it includes only those simple natures that share the common nature *extension*. The sensory idea of the Sun, on the other hand, is confused since it comprises some simple natures that entail *extension*, while including some simple natures that entail *thinking*. We might say that the idea "mixes together" simple natures from the two mutually exclusive basic classes.

Seeing Necessary Connections

In the *Rules*, Descartes introduced two ways by which a mind comes to know something. The first is what he called *intuition*, and the second is what he referred to as *deduction*. (AT X 365-370; CSM I 12-15) Intuition is an *immediate* cognitive insight that comes in a single "moment" of experience. This insight is sometimes cast as one's "seeing" or understanding the necessary connection between simple natures constituting the content of the idea. Sometimes Descartes suggested that this insight *is* the compelling of the will—as when the will *affirms* the connection. It could certainly be Descartes's view, then, that the understanding of the connection (seeing the truth) and the will's assenting (to this truth) are only conceptually (or perhaps only modally) distinct—they could turn out to be really one and the same event. Be that as it may, he contrasted intuition with deduction, which is the cognitive insight into how two "moments" of experience are necessarily connected—into what we might think of as an *inference*. Deduction is a kind of discursive reasoning. He wrote:

The Search for Truth and Certainty | 51

> Hence we are distinguishing mental intuition from certain deduction on the grounds that we are aware of a movement or a sort of sequence in the latter but not in the former, and also because immediate self-evidence is not required for deduction, as it is for intuition. (AT X 370; CSM I 15)

A good example of deduction is offered in the Fifth Meditation. Descartes supposed that if something is a quadrilateral, it is inscribable in a circle. He then assumed that a rhombus is a quadrilateral. From these two claims, "[I]t will be necessary for me to admit that a rhombus can be inscribed in a circle," despite the fact that this conclusion "is patently false." (AT VII 67; CSM II 46) The insight of the necessary connection here is between the first two suppositions and the conclusion. If the supposed claims were true, the conclusion would have to be true, too. Descartes was quick to note, however, that the conclusion is false, in which case at least one of the supposed claims had to be false. The first supposition—*If something is a quadrilateral, it is inscribable in a circle*—turns out to be the false claim. His point was that if the assumptions *were* true, then the conclusion could not be false. The trouble with deduction, he said, is the lack of any guarantee that the assumptions, the starting point in our line of reasoning, are true. Intuition will be different. Not only will it not involve "moving" from one claim to another (or from one idea to another), but its starting point will be *given* as true.

In the *Principles*, Descartes listed four claims that look to be intuition-like in the sense introduced in the *Rules* (he referred to them as *axiom*-like), though they could easily be mistaken to be instances of deduction. Here's the list (which isn't exhaustive):

> *Nothing comes from nothing,*
> *It is impossible for the same thing to be and not to be at the same time,*
> *What is done cannot be undone,*
> *He who thinks cannot but exist while he thinks.* (AT VIIIA 23-24; CSM I 209)

Let's take this last one since Descartes famously appealed to it as the first solid thing one could know, given one was entertaining even the most exaggerated kind of doubt; it would be the first *necessarily* true claim one would discover if philosophizing in the proper order. (*Principles*, AT VIIIA 8; CSM I 196)

Let's recall the famous phrase: *I think, therefore I am* (though widely attributed to Descartes, several critics claimed it could be found earlier, in the work of Augustine). Within the context of Descartes's work, the expression first appeared in 1637, in *Discourse on the Method* (1637): "*I am thinking, therefore I exist.*" (AT VI 32; CSM I 127) He wrote there that even while trying to imagine that everything he believed was false, he couldn't manage to make this phrase false. "I noticed that while I was trying thus to think everything false, it was necessary that I, who was thinking this, was something." (*Ibid.*) A bit later, he noted that the truth of this insight stems directly from his clearly seeing that "in order to think it is necessary to exist." (AT VII 33; CSM I 127) In the opening of the Second Meditation, he again worked out this insight. Scholars have referred to this famous reflection as the *cogito* (the Latin *cogito* means *I think* or *I am thinking*). To keep our discussion from getting too wordy, we'll use this term to refer to the immediate insight that it is necessary—that when I think, I exist. The *cogito* is an answer to the skeptical questions he raised in the First Meditation, where Descartes had worked up a most exaggerated kind of doubt—the possibility that an infinitely powerful evil being designed him in such a way that even in the simplest of cases, as when adding two and three and getting five, he would go wrong and would be deceived into believing something to be true that was, in fact, false. (AT VII 21-23; CSM II 14-15)

At the opening of the Second Meditation, Descartes had assigned a special epistemic status to a belief that could not be doubted. About the ancient Greek philosopher, Archimedes, Descartes wrote:

> Archimedes used to demand just one firm and immovable point in order to shift the entire earth; so I too can hope

for great things if I manage to find just one thing, however slight, that is certain and unshakeable. (AT VII 24; CSM II 16)

Here, a belief that could not be doubted would be analogous to the immovable Archimedean point. The idea is that one can lift something of great weight with a lever. An important element of such a machine is the fulcrum: the fixed and immovable point that allows the lever to do its thing. Descartes's insight was that one belief that cannot be doubted even if it is mundane, could be used, like the fulcrum, to do some heavy epistemological lifting. He could build a system of knowledge around such a belief. Although any one of the axiom-like items listed above would do here, Descartes said that when doing philosophy in the proper order, one will land upon the *cogito* first—which is expressed in the above claim *He who thinks cannot but exist while he thinks*, as in the famous phrase *I think, therefore I am*. (AT VIII 7; CSM I 195) So, for Descartes, the *cogito* served as the philosophical Archimedean point. Such a belief is more like an intuition than a deduction.

Now, contrast the immediate insight of the *cogito* with what Descartes said at the end of the Second Meditation, when he was entertaining his thoughts on the nature or essence of body, and how that is known. The body under discussion is a piece of wax:

> For if I judge that the wax exists from the fact that I see it, clearly this same fact entails much more evidently that I myself also exist. It is possible that what I see is not really the wax; it is possible that I do not even have eyes with which to see anything. But when I see, or think I see (I am not here distinguishing between the two), it is simply not possible that I who am now thinking am not something. By the same token, if I judge that the wax exists from the fact that I touch it, the same result follows, namely that I exist. If I judge that it exists from the fact that I imagine it, or for any other reason, exactly the same thing follows. (AT VII 33; CSM II 22)

Given that *seeing*, *touching*, *imagining*, and so on, are acts of the mind, then if you believe that a body exists, say, based on your seeing or feeling it, then that commits you to believing that your mind, the thing doing the seeing and feeling, exists. If you believe that a body exists based on your imagining it, then that commits you to believing that your mind, the thing doing the imagining, exists. Even so, Descartes was quick to note that our starting point here—that the body exists—may not be true. But that doesn't matter in this case. What matters is our seeing that the one thing entails or presupposes the other: the claim that a body exists, based on your touching it, entails or presupposes the claim that your mind exists. Since the entailment (or presupposition) relation is there, but the starting point isn't given as true, the above is an example of deduction, not intuition. By contrast, the *cogito* is an example of intuition. Let's see how this is so.

In the Second Meditation, Descartes argued, supposing that such a deceiver is deliberately and constantly deceiving him:

> In that case I too undoubtedly exist, if he is deceiving me; and let him deceive me as much as he can, he will never bring it about that I am nothing so long as I think that I am something. So after considering everything very thoroughly, I must finally conclude that this proposition, *I am, I exist*, is necessarily true whenever it is put forward by me or conceived in my mind. (AT VII 25; CSM II 17)

The insight as told here goes as follows: Suppose that "I exist" is true if, and only if, it picks out a fact in the world, namely the fact that I exist. "I exist" is false, then, if I don't exist. Now, let's say that this evil deceiver wants to deceive me about "I exist." That is, it wants to get me to believe that "I exist" is true when it is in fact false. Well, for that to succeed, the truth would have to be that I don't exist, for that is what needs to be factual in order for "I exist" to be false. But in order for this deceiver to trick *me* into believing that "I exist," it will have to be true that I exist. Otherwise, *who* is the deceiver fooling? The success of this case requires, then, that I exist *and* that I not exist, all at the same time, which is impossible. But my existing and not existing, all at the same time, is *inconceivable*. So, the truth of "I exist" is guaranteed whenever I think or believe it.

That something is inconceivable, or impossible, can be contrasted with something that is necessary. *I exist and do not exist at the same time* is inconceivable. *That I exist whenever I think* is necessary. Notice that Descartes employed both ways of talking when formulating the *cogito*. Notice, too, that these are two of the axiom-like (intuition-like) claims listed earlier: *It is impossible for the same thing to be and not to be at the same time*, and *He who thinks cannot but exist while he thinks*.

Now, why isn't the *cogito* an instance of deduction? After all, Descartes used the typical conclusion indicator "therefore," which indicates an inference has been drawn. This is how Descartes responded to critics who had insisted that he was involved in deduction:

> And when we become aware that we are thinking things, this is a primary notion which is not derived by means of any syllogism. When someone says "I am thinking, therefore I am, or I exist," he does not deduce existence from thought by means of a syllogism, but recognizes it as something self-evident by a simple intuition of the mind. This is clear from the fact that if he were deducing it by means of a syllogism, he would have to have had previous knowledge of the major premise "Everything which thinks is, or exists"; yet in fact he learns it from experiencing in his own case that it is impossible that he should think without existing. (AT VII 140; CSM II 100)

A syllogism is a form of argument. Descartes noted here that "I am thinking, therefore I exist" is *not* an argument, though it may look like one. It is not an instance of deduction. Rather, as he tried to explain to his critics, seeing that it is necessary, that it *must* be the case, that one exists whenever one is thinking, is an *immediate* insight—it is an intuition. Another way to put this is: It is inconceivable that I think but don't exist. One could not even imagine that it was true that one was thinking but false that one existed (while thinking). This insight, the "seeing" of this necessary connection (whether positively or negatively put) is what will account for the idea's being *clear*. But in addition to seeing the necessary connection, it is the case that, while thinking, one would be immediately aware that one is thinking. Thus, the "starting point" here, which is expressed as *I am thinking*, is given as true. These two things tell us that the *cogito* is an intuition and not an instance of deduction.

So, the *big* question is: What warrants our trusting such an insight? To be sure, you cannot conceive the scenario in which you are thinking but don't exist (for that would mean you are thinking that you exist and don't exist, which is impossible). Could your inability to conceive such a scenario actually be an obstacle to your having knowledge here? What guarantee do we have that this perception can *never* lead us astray? Descartes spent a great deal of time addressing these questions in the *Discourse*, the *Meditations*, and the *Principles*.

In all three works, he ruled out the trustworthiness of his ideas that appear to have their origin in the senses. He did this by showing that they—their truth—can be easily doubted. Although Descartes played fast and loose with the notions of *idea*, *proposition*, and *belief*, we can tidy things up for him by allowing the following: a proposition expresses the content of an idea, whereas a belief is your holding that what this proposition expresses is true. So, "I think, therefore I exist" can be understood as expressing the content of an idea, where the belief would be that what is expressed is true. So, instead of muddying the waters by talk of doubting an idea, we can make progress if we clean things up and instead talk of doubting a belief. The notion of *doubt* here will be understood as our being uncertain that the belief is true. In the Second Meditation, Descartes wrote that he *couldn't* doubt the belief "I am thinking, therefore I exist." Fine. But what is the criterion for doubting a belief? Descartes suggested that we can doubt a belief if we can tell a story in which the belief is false. As just noted, he doubted the trustworthiness of his sensory beliefs (rooted in ideas that appear to have their origin in the senses) by telling stories in which they are false. What might such a notion of doubt tell us about the *cogito*, and, just as importantly, about its role in Descartes's philosophy?

Let's begin with those sensory beliefs (beliefs related to sensory experience). Although there are subtleties here, we can get a sense of the utility of Descartes's notion of doubt by focusing on a story that allows us to doubt all beliefs originating in or from the senses. Descartes noted, for instance, that there is no recognizable sign by which we can tell for sure whether we are awake or are dreaming. (AT VII 19; CSM II 13) Since this is the case, it is *possible* that although you believe you're awake and sitting here reading this book, the fact is that you are dreaming this—but just don't know it. So, if you're dreaming, then the belief that you're awake, or the belief that you're holding this book in your hands, and so on, are false beliefs—for neither of those things is really happening. You see your good friend Ken off in the distance and call to him. He walks up to you, and you tell him about the book dream—but *Bam!*—you wake up and realize that this scene was just a dream. The belief that you were talking to Ken, that Ken had walked up to you, and so on, are all false. Now, Descartes wasn't trying to convince you that you are dreaming, or that you are always dreaming. Rather, he was making the case that since there is no sure sign that you are awake or dreaming, then it's always possible that you're dreaming, in which case the beliefs you have about everything that you are currently sensing (seeing, feeling, hearing, and so on) might be false. The point is that since we can tell a story in which such beliefs are false, they can be doubted. And if they can be doubted, they are not intuitions.

Descartes said that even though such sensory beliefs can be called into doubt, other beliefs, such as adding two and three and getting five, appear to be undoubtable, at least not in light of the dream story. For, whether awake or dreaming, two added to three is five.

But what if our minds were designed by an infinitely powerful evil being? Couldn't this being have designed us so that there is simply a limit to what stories we can tell—a limit to what we can and cannot conceive? To answer this question, we'll have to keep it in mind that in order to doubt a belief, it will have to be possible for us to tell a story in which the belief is false. So, is the story about the infinitely powerful evil being possible? Is it a story that we can tell? Can we really imagine a case—the case in question—in which an evil being has created us such that even in the simplest matters, like adding two and three and getting five, we go wrong? For, if such were imaginable, we would be in a position to doubt even mathematics (or beliefs related to mathematics).

Descartes reminded himself of his idea of an infinite being (we considered that in the previous two chapters). This idea, he argued, was *prior* to his idea of himself as a finite substance. It is prior in the sense that the idea of a finite being is derived from the idea of an infinite being. To use our earlier terminology, the idea of a finite being presupposes that of an infinite being. Suffice it to say here, as a reminder, that this relationship—the relationship a finite being has to the infinite—is the basis for the claim that your mind (and any finite being, for that matter) has its origin in the infinite. In the story of the deceiver, the being trying to trick us must be both infinitely powerful (so infinite) and evil. This being, the infinite being, is taken as the origin of our mind, its inner workings, its faculty of reason, and so on. The question is: is such a being possible? Descartes argued that such a thing is internally *contradictory*. That is, an infinite-*evil* being is as contradictory as a square-circle, or as a thing that exists and doesn't exist at the same time. Since this is so, and we cannot conceive such a being, then there is no story to tell after all. The upshot is that we cannot conceive the case in which our faculty of reason, the faculty responsible for the insight into necessary connections, is unreliable or can lead us astray. Let's briefly look at this and bring this chapter to a close.

Descartes said that in order to understand what it is to be *deceived*, we must consider two conceptual items: *being* and *non-being*. (AT VII 53f; CSM II 37f, AT V 9; CSMK III 316, AT V 357;

CSMK III 378) Let's say that I want to deceive you into believing that I have a coin in my hand. To understand this as an instance of *deception*, you are basically considering the coin in my hand as an instance of *being*. The deception occurs if I can get you to think that there is *being* in my hand when in fact there isn't. Likewise, I might try to get you to think that nothing (non-being) is in my hand (that I have nothing in my closed hand) when in fact there is something there (being), like that coin. Recall that *finite* being also requires these two items: being and non-being. A finite being is a being that is limited. The limits are understood in terms of non-being, in something taken away. "[I]n order to conceive a finite being," Descartes noted, "I have to take away something from the general notion of being." (AT V 356; CSMK III 377) This "general notion of being" is the idea of being *without* limits–the idea of infinite being. Notice that the notions of *finite being* and *deception* are closely allied: both require for their construction being and non-being. The point here is that the infinite being can in no way be tied to limitation or defect. In an Augustinian view, *being* is associated epistemologically with *truth* and morally with *goodness*; non-being is associated epistemologically with *falsity* and morally with *evil*. Evil is simply a privation or lack of being. As we noted at the opening of this chapter, Descartes had adopted a version of this view. Now, since evil is associated with non-being, the very conception of deception cannot be applied to God (the infinite being), for the infinite being is *all* being, and has absolutely no ties to non-being. In other words, an *evil-infinite being* is a contradiction. And so, although it may have looked promising before we began our philosophical analysis, it turns out that stories in which mathematical beliefs are false cannot be told. That is, we cannot imagine such a story. Since this is so, we were actually never in a position to doubt them. They were among the Archimedean-like beliefs all along. But more importantly, our not being able to tell the story of the all-powerful-evil being secures for us the *cogito*, which, recall, is the first such Archimedean-like belief we run across when doing philosophy in the proper order.

In the Third Meditation, Descartes foreshadowed this insight:

> But what about when I was considering something very simple and straightforward in arithmetic or geometry, for example that two and three added together make five, and so on. Did I not see at least these things clearly enough to affirm their truth? Indeed, the only reason for my later judgment that they were open to doubt was that it occurred to me that perhaps some God could have given me a nature such that I was deceived even in matters which seemed most evident…But in order to remove even this slight reason for doubt, as soon as the opportunity arises I must examine whether there is a God, and, if there is, whether he can be a deceiver. (AT VII 36; CSM II 25)

The upshot, as we know, is that he would show that God exists, and as we just learned, that God, by God's very nature, cannot be a deceiver. How does this guarantee that our faculty of reason is trustworthy? How can we be sure that when we add two and three that the answer really is five? How can we be sure that when I see the necessary connection between *I think* and *I exist* that it really must be true that whenever I think, I exist? Here's how: Remember that a finite mind has its origin in the infinite being. So, your cognitive faculties have the infinite being as their author. If God gave you defective faculties, which led you astray and caused you to believe false things even when used properly, God would be a deceiver. But, God isn't a deceiver (in fact, God *cannot* be a deceiver). According to Descartes, this means that your God-given faculties, if properly employed, will never lead you astray, and will never cause you to believe false things.

The Circle

Some critics—for instance, Antoine Arnauld and Pierre

Gassendi—expressed concern about Descartes's arrival at the trustworthiness of our faculty of reason. Here's Arnauld's concern: Let's say that we are questioning the reliability of our faculty of reason—whether it can lead us astray; whether it can be trusted. You'd be making a pretty big mistake to then use that very same faculty in answering that question. Arnauld was basically saying that if you're questioning whether the faculty of reason is reliable, you can't seriously rely on it to see whether it is reliable. Arnauld's criticism specifically was focused on Descartes's use of clear and distinct perception to establish that God exists and is no deceiver, and then applying this result to establish the reliability of clear and distinct perception. This line of reasoning, Arnauld suggested, was circular. The analysis offered in the previous section suggests that Arnauld's criticism would be worrisome only if we could conceive the case in which our faculty of reason, when used properly, could go wrong and lead us astray. But we cannot conceive the case. This is so because the idea of an infinitely powerful evil being is a logical contradiction.

Certainty

Descartes recognized two kinds of certainty: *metaphysical* and *moral*. In this section, we'll focus on the first kind.

He seemed to have two formulations of metaphysical certainty available to him. The first is what we might call a *negative* formulation, the second a *positive* formulation. They are:

> **Negative**: You are certain of *p*, or certain that *p* is true, if, and only if, you see that not-*p* is impossible.
>
> **Positive**: You are certain of *p*, or certain that *p* is true, if, and only if, you are (your will is) compelled to assent to *p*.

In connection to what was said in the previous section (about the circle), Descartes posited:

> Now if this conviction is so firm that it is impossible for us ever to have any reason for doubting what we are convinced of, then there are no further questions for us to ask: we have everything that we could reasonably want...For the supposition which we are making here is of a conviction so firm that it is quite incapable of being destroyed; and such a conviction is clearly the same as the most perfect certainty. (AT VII 144; CSM II 103)

Recall that in order to doubt a belief, you had to be able to tell a story in which the belief was false. This didn't show that the belief was really false, of course, it only established the *possibility* of its being false. The belief, in other words, was *doubtable*. The other side of this, then, is that if you could not tell such a story, then the belief could not be doubted. As we saw in the last section, since we could not tell a story in which our faculty of reason could go wrong (when used properly), we had no grounds for doubting its reliability.

The above are the nuts and bolts of Descartes's epistemology and how it related to his metaphysics. Although Descartes entertained the arguments of the skeptics, he was no skeptic himself. Clearly, he thought that a thorough philosophical analysis would reveal that the mind is perfectly suited to know the truth: it will have clear and distinct ideas. As should be clear from this chapter, the mind's being so suited is underwritten by God, the mind's creator, whose nature is incompatible with being a deceiver. As we now turn to Descartes's view about the body, we'll see that this theme continues because even the laws of nature are expressions of the divine will. There is no aspect of Descartes's philosophy that isn't ultimately underwritten by an appeal to God.

4. Body

According to Descartes's ontology, *body* is one of the two finite substances that exist in the cosmos. (AT VII 14; CSM II 10) The other, as discussed in Chapter 2, is *mind*. The nature or essence of body, or corporeal substance, is *extension* in three dimensions: length, breadth, and depth. In the Second Set of Replies he said:

> The substance which is the immediate subject of local extension and of the accidents which presuppose extension, such as shape, position, local motion and so on, is called *body*. (AT VII 161; CSM II 114)

As he later wrote in the *Principles*, extension is the principal attribute of body. (AT VIIIA 25; CSM I 210) Being solid, hard, impenetrable, and so on, are not essential features of body. They are modes. So, for instance, what we call *space* is in essence no different from any "solid" body moving from one location to another. Space is body, too, since it is extended.

You've no doubt noticed that in some places we have used just the term *body* to refer to this corporeal substance, while elsewhere we have used the term with the indefinite article–*a* body. Space is body; but it isn't *a* body (unless you mean to cast it as *res extensa*, the extension of the entire material reality). But if we limit ourselves to some region of space, we might find ourselves talking of the Sun, for instance, where we'd very likely take this to be *a* body. But even here, when we construct the idea of the Sun by way of astronomical principles, where the Sun is now exhibited as a sphere in motion, this new idea *could* be used to simply represent finite body–finite corporeal substance–an idea that represents a shaped thing that is extended. Of course, this sort of "stripped down" idea of the Moon or of a coffee table could be used to represent finite body too. Notice that neither the clear and distinct *idea* of body nor the clear and distinct *idea* of *a* body includes the simple natures *color*, *heat*, and the like. They include the simple nature *extension* and only those simple natures that presuppose *extension*. This would be the sort of stripped-down version just mentioned. So, we'd probably be hard-pressed to refer to such a stripped-down idea as the idea of the Sun or the Moon, but such an idea would be perfectly suited, according to Descartes, to be referred to as an idea of body.

Whether Descartes took there to be many *bodies* or only one *body* has been a matter of contention among scholars. The many-bodies view contends that there are numerous distinct corporeal *substances*; the one-body view holds that there is only one corporeal *substance*. The one-body approach accounts for our perceiving many bodies by understanding those bodies, such as the Sun and Moon, as being only modally distinct. They are simply different modal "systems," we might say, that reside in different regions of the one corporeal substance—*res extensa*. Thus, both the Sun and Moon are essentially the same—both are essentially extended—varying only modally, where by "modally" we are referring to the modes of extension such as shape, size, and the like. You might recall that in an earlier chapter it was noted that this was Spinoza's take on Descartes. There are ways of showing that both views are right, and that they are not necessarily at odds with one another. We'll show some of this by chapter's end.

Divisibility

Descartes said that body is divisible, and indefinitely so, by its very nature. Any body, no matter how small, can be divided, and the remaining extended bits, which are also bodies, can be divided as well, and the remaining extended bits (which are bodies too) can also be divided, and so on *ad infinitum*. This can lead to a philosophical problem because, according to Descartes, body is a *substance*, and a substance is "incorruptible, and cannot ever cease to exist." (AT VII 14; CSM II 10) Now, in the period in which Descartes lived corruptibility was typically understood in terms of divisibility. That is, we corrupt a thing by dividing it into bits, scattering them so that the thing divided no longer exists (as the thing prior to division). Take a piece of chalk. We divide it in half, and in half again, and so on, and then take the "powder" that is left (tiny bits that constituted the previously divided piece of chalk) and scatter it about. That piece of chalk is no more; it has been corrupted. To be sure, bits of the previously divided piece of chalk remain, but they no longer form the thing that we took to be our initial piece of chalk. Annihilation, by contrast, would mean that nothing of the chalk, not even the bits, remained. Annihilation can only happen by way of God's withholding what was sometimes called God's *concurrence*. So, there are two ways that the chalk could be taken out of existence: corruption and annihilation. The former is a natural process (it can occur in nature), the latter a divine act. Descartes theorized that body, understood as a finite substance, cannot be taken out of existence by any natural process, though bodies such as that piece of chalk or the Sun can be taken out of existence (understood as that piece of chalk or the Sun), but that would have to occur by way of division and scattering.

So, if body is divisible by its very nature, why couldn't we corrupt it? This is where Descartes's view gets tricky. Recall from previous chapters what was said about things like the Sun. They would count as instances of body. Each individual body has the very same nature: *extension*. So, with respect to their nature, bodies do not differ. Consider again that piece of chalk. Let's say that we divide it in half. The halves are separated by what? Well, they are separated by space. But space is as much *body* as is the piece of chalk and any of its bits. So, although we have divided the chalk and have separated one half from the other, what separates them is still *body*. In a general sense, we have not divided *body*, but have divided some *instance* of body, and have separated the divided parts by another instance of body. In fact, we could never divide and then *separate* two halves of *body* in this general sense (as simply an extended thing). Let's consider doing that—dividing space, say, in half and then separating the two divided halves of space from one another. What stands between them? Nothing? Well, if nothing, then the two halves aren't really separated at all. They are still contiguous and touch. If space separates them, then although we may count these particular regions of space to be separated, they are nevertheless separated by space. In that sense, we still haven't *really* divided the two regions of space; we've simply *inserted* space between space. "Divided" space would be no different from the space "undivided."

In light of this, scholars have argued that there seem to be two senses of "divisibility" here. The first is what we might call *real divisibility*. This would be aligned with *real distinction*, which was discussed in earlier chapters. Remember that two things, A and B, are said to be really distinct, if, and only if, we can conceive the nature of A independently of the nature of B, and vice versa. This, Descartes noted, supports the further claim that really distinct things are *substances*, and can exist independently of one another. The second sense of "divisibility" is what we might call *modal divisibility*. This would be aligned with *modal distinction*. Given these two senses, consider again that piece of chalk. We divide it in half. Now, are the two halves really distinct? No. They are not really distinct since we cannot conceive the nature of the one half independently of the nature of the other. Why can't we? Both have the same nature: *extension*. If real divisibility requires that the divided items be really distinct, then the piece of chalk is not *really divisible*. The one half has a shape and a location, as does the other half. Since we understand the distinction between them in terms of modes and not natures, they are at best modally distinct. If modal divisibility requires that the divided item be modally distinct, then the piece of chalk is *modally divisible*.

Therefore, in one sense *body* cannot be corrupted, but in another sense, *a* body can be corrupted. In terms of real divisibility, body cannot be corrupted since the parts post division are not really distinct. In this sense, body is a substance. By contrast, divided parts, in terms of modal divisibility, body (or better, *a* body) can be corrupted since the parts post division are modally distinct (and can be subsequently scattered). This would be the sense in which body is *divisible* by its very nature. If we take Descartes this way, then body can be said to be divisible by its nature—it is modally divisible—and yet body can be said to be a substance or to be incorruptible since it is not really divisible. What is more, with respect to concerns over substantiality and real divisibility, there is only *one* body; whereas with respect to concerns over things like the Sun or the Moon, or that piece of chalk and what we're calling modal divisibility, there are *many* bodies. This allows both interpretations of Descartes—the one body and the many bodies interpretations—to be understood as being consistent.

Does Body Exist?

In early parts of many of Descartes's works, when trying to establish a ground for the reliability of the faculty of reason, he notoriously doubted the existence of body, that is, the existence of material reality. But when we consider the big picture, we find that this doubt was feigned. He really wasn't a skeptic about the existence of a material world that exists independently of the mind. You might recall that in the Second Meditation, when discussing what we called *deduction*, Descartes said that if, in our judgment, a body exists (such as a piece of wax) based upon our seeing or feeling it, this perception entails that the mind, the thing doing the seeing and feeling, also exists. (AT VII 33; CSM II 22) Of course, this doesn't prove that this body exists. Rather, Descartes's point was that *if* we say that it does, then we're logically committed to the claim that the mind exists. You might also recall that in the Third Meditation, Descartes offered the proof for the existence of an infinite substance, God. This proof turned on an analysis of the level of objective reality contained in his idea of God. He reasoned that since the level of formal reality that his mind possessed was not great enough to be the origin of the objective reality in this idea, there must exist some being that does possess the required level of formal reality, and that was an infinite substance.

When Descartes devised a proof for the existence of body in the Sixth Meditation, he posited that it would be the idea that exhibits to him an extended finite substance. In terms of the level of objective reality contained in this idea, which demonstrates the level of a finite substance, Descartes noted that the level of formal reality possessed by his mind is great enough to be the origin of the objective reality here. So, were we to narrow down our analysis just to an examination of the *level* of objective reality contained in the idea of body, nothing would require us to claim that there is a corporeal substance existing independently of the mind. The mind can be the origin of the level of objective reality contained in the idea of body. This was remarkably different from his analysis of the idea of God. But thinking back to his analysis of his idea of the wax in the Second Meditation, Descartes noticed that the idea of body shows a certain collection of what we've been calling simple natures—*shape, size, motion*, and so on—which presuppose *extension*. These constitute what a body *is*. When thinking about body, these are the very things one thinks about. In contrast to his analysis of the idea of God, his interpretation of the idea of body turned away from worrying about the level of objective reality, and focused instead on the simple natures—the objective *beings*—constituting the content of the idea of body.

In the Third Meditation, right before the proof for God's existence, Descartes introduced the principle suggesting that ultimately the objective reality contained in our *primary* ideas—the "first and most important ones"—must have its origin in the formal reality possessed by things. (AT VII 42; CSM II 29) He said:

> Now it is manifest by the natural light that there must be at least as much <reality> in the efficient and total cause as in the effect of that cause. For where, I ask, could the effect get its reality from, if not from the cause? And how could the cause give it to the effect unless it possessed it?...A stone,

for example, which previously did not exist, cannot begin to exist unless it is produced by something which contains, either formally or eminently everything to be found in the stone; similarly, heat cannot be produced in an object which was not previously hot, except by something of at least the same order <or degree or kind> of perfection as heat, and so on. But it is also true that the *idea* of heat, or of a stone, cannot exist in me unless it is put there by some cause which contains at least as much reality as I conceive to be in the heat or in the stone. (Third Meditation, AT VII 40-41; CSM II 28)

To understand what he wrote here, the reference to *formal* and *eminent* should first be explained. So, let's do that.

This is a medieval distinction that Descartes borrowed. The gist of the distinction is as follows: When a cause possesses the property it is said *to give* to the effect, the possession is said to be *formal*. We might define it thus (where **A** and **B** are things, and **p** is a property):

> **A** is said to possess **p** formally if, and only if, (1) **A** causes **B** to possess **p**, and (2) it is true that **A** *is* **p**.

Let **A** be *fire*, **B** be *water* (in a pot), and **p** be the property *heat*. Suppose that the fire is said to be the cause of the water's being hot. In the case in which the fire is said to give to (or to produce in) the water (in the pot) the property heat, and it also true that fire is hot, the fire (the cause) is said to possess heat *formally*.

We might define *eminent* possession thus:

> **A** is said to possess **p** eminently if, and only if, (1) **A** causes **B** to possess **p**, and (2) it is not true that **A** *is* **p**.

Here, let **A** be *fire*, **B** be a *piece of wood*, and **p** be the property *black*. Suppose that the fire is said to be the cause of the wood's becoming black. In the case in which fire is said to produce blackness in the wood, and yet it is false to say that fire is black, the fire (the cause) is said to possess black *eminently*.

Return to the idea of body. It exhibits something that is *shaped, sized, extended,* and so on. As Descartes argued in the Sixth Meditation, the analysis of his ideas of body and mind shows that body and mind are really distinct. That is, he demonstrated that we could conceive the nature of the one independently of the nature of the other. Now, if his mind is the cause of what is exhibited to him in the idea of body, and mind is by its very nature thinking and not extended, then the mind at best would possess extension (and the other simple natures that presuppose extension) only *eminently*. How so? Well, although it will be true to say that the mind (its formal reality) is the cause of the idea's possessing objective being, it will nevertheless be *false* to say that the mind is extended (shaped, sized, and so on). This is like the case of the fire producing blackness in the wood. But in this case, the idea exhibits something that is *radically* different from a mind. Such an idea could only be said to be false, since it so radically *misrepresents* the object it is said to exhibit.

What is more, Descartes found "absolutely no connection" between these "corporeal" modes and anything that presupposes thinking. (AT VII 76; CSM II 53) In light of the discussion in Chapter 3, Descartes appeared to be committed to saying that this idea is *obscure*. Of course, given that it includes simple natures that presuppose extension, not thinking, where extension and thinking are "in some way opposites" (AT VII 13; CSM II 10), and yet this very idea was taken to exhibit a *mind*, a thing that was, according to the idea, extended, would also look to commit Descartes to say that this idea was *confused*. It would be confused given that it included simple natures from the two principal (and mutually exclusive) classes of the enumeration: the class of thinking things and the class of extended things.

But, as a matter of fact, this idea nevertheless shows a connection, and a necessary one at that, between the simple natures *shape, size,* and *extension*. Since this is so, the idea, if taken to represent a corporeal substance, would be said to be clear. And since it would include only those simple natures that presuppose extension (they are included in the class of extended things), the idea would also be said to be distinct. So, is the idea of *mind*, in which case the idea is obscure and confused, or is the idea of *body*, that is, of something really distinct from mind, in which case the idea is clear and distinct? If we say that the idea exhibits *mind*, then we're claiming that a clear and distinct idea—here, the idea of body—is *false!* Since Descartes rejected the possibility that clear and distinct ideas are false (AT VII 35; CSM II 24), it will follow that the idea is of *body*, and is not an idea of mind.

Descartes recognized only four possible causes of the clear and distinct idea of body: God, his own mind, some other finite mind, or body. He argued:

> This substance [i.e. that which causes in him the idea of body] is either a body, that is, a corporeal nature, in which case it will contain formally <and in fact> everything which is to be found objectively <or representatively> in the ideas; or else it is God, or some creature more noble than a body, in which case it will contain eminently whatever is to be found in the ideas. But since God is not a deceiver, it is quite clear that he does not transmit the idea to me either directly or indirectly, via some creature which contains the objective reality of the idea not formally but only eminently. For God has given me no faculty at all for recognizing any such source for these ideas; on the contrary, he has given me a great propensity to believe that they are produced by corporeal things. So I do not see how God could be understood to be anything but a deceiver if the idea were transmitted from a source other than corporeal things. It follows that corporeal things exist. (AT VII 79–80; CSM II 55)

To account for the idea of body, what it exhibits, in light of having established clarity and distinctness as indicators of truth, and having shown that God exists, is no deceiver, and is the origin of his faculty of reason, Descartes concluded that body exists (or, as he noted in the above passage, that bodies exist).

Body, Number, and the Intelligibility of Mathematics

In the *Principles*, Descartes said that the distinction between *number* and *the things numbered* is merely *conceptual*. Here, he specifically noted that by "things" he meant *bodies*. Numbers are ways of conceiving bodies—or a way of conceiving extension *divided*, where the regions divided by way of motion are taken to be instances of body. As noted earlier, instances of body would be modally distinct. Descartes went even further, saying that number "is unintelligible without some extended substance." (AT VIIIA 44-45; CSM I 226) This does more than to suggest that extension is a necessary condition for the intelligibility of numbers. So, no extension (no body), no numbers (that is, numbers are unintelligible). Being a "way of conceiving" body is another way of referring to intelligibility. Although numbers may be inhabitants of a mind, their intelligibility depends on extension. If extension did not exist, they would be unintelligible, which is another way of saying that they could not be thought. And, if they could not be thought, they, too, wouldn't exist. The point to emphasize here is that *number*, like *shape*, presupposes *extension*. In fact, all ideas of body (all ways of conceiving body), insofar as they are ideas, depend on the mind, but insofar as they are *of* or represent *body*, depend on body (*extension*).

In the Fifth Set of Replies, Descartes told French philosopher Pierre Gassendi (1592-1655) that the *shapes* studied by geometers are not substances themselves, but are "boundaries within which a substance is contained." (AT VII 381; CSM II 262) Thus, the Sun, which is spherical in shape, may contain a substance—the extended substance—but that substance, it would seem, is the very same one contained by the Earth's shape, which is also spherical. The difference between the Earth and Sun isn't their nature or their shape, but their size, location relative to other shaped-things, and so on. The term "modal system" was used earlier. The *size, shape, location,* and *local motion* of the Earth, we might say, form a modal system. These modes relate to one another in such a way that they "travel" as a unit—the unit, in our example, called "Earth." The *size, shape, location,* and *local motion* of the Sun also form a modal system, which we call (the) "Sun." Therefore, we might say that individuated bodies are, in fact, modal systems, each modifying one and the same substance, extension (or *res extensa,* the *extended thing*). This, recall, was Spinoza's take on Descartes's view.

In his *Discourse on Metaphysics,* Spinoza's friend, German philosopher Gottfried Leibniz (1646-1716), argued that perfections (or *actual* properties) must admit of a highest degree. Knowledge and power are perfections since they admit of a highest degree. Here, he seems to mean that there is a degree of knowledge that cannot be surpassed by "more" knowledge. This holds for power too. There is a degree of power that cannot be surpassed by "more" power. Leibniz argued that God, in being absolutely perfect, possesses all perfections, and possesses them in the highest degree. (*Discourse on Metaphysics,* Art. 1) Since shape and number do not admit of a highest degree (for any given shape there is always one with more sides; likewise, for any given number, there is always one greater), they are not perfections. It follows that God does not possess them. This strongly suggests that in a world in which there exists *only* God, only the Divine being, there are no numbers and there are no shapes. And, this suggests that in such a world there would be no mathematics—arithmetic and geometry, for example. That there are numbers and shapes, then, implies that there must be something (other than God) that accounts for their intelligibility (i.e., their being intelligible to finite minds). Descartes's view seems to be that extension (body) is the finite substance that accounts for this.

Mathematics, then, although a salient expression of the intellect, depends nevertheless on the existence of body. No body, no mathematics—for, as we know, Descartes argued that without extension (body) number and shape are unintelligible. As we learned earlier, Descartes also claimed that an attribute is presupposed in our experience of a mode; and that an existing substance is presupposed in our experience of an attribute. (AT VIIIA 25; CSM I 210) So, if we perceive two spherical things, we perceive *modes*. These modes (or our perceptions of them) presuppose some *attribute*, which in this case is the principal attribute *extension*. Our perception of this attribute presupposes an existing substance. The intelligibility of shape and number, in other words, presupposes (entails) an existent corporeal substance. This view, it seems, led Descartes to believe in an internal connection between the material world and mathematics. And, this insight would lead him to begin considering how one might go about "mathematizing" the material world stripped of colors, sounds, smells, and the like; a world of shaped-things in motion. This insight into the mathematization of our experience of the material world is part of the story of the development of modern physics. Let's now turn to this concept—in the next chapter we'll not only get a clearer understanding of Descartes's attempt to *mathematize* our experience of bodies, but also get a clearer picture of how he attempted to go a step further and *mechanize* life—that is, how he tried to show that *living* things were nothing more than complex machines—bodies with sophisticated internal structures.

5. Physics and the Mechanization of Life

The English word "physics" has its origin in the ancient Greek word *fusiz* (pronounced *phoozees*). The word originally denoted the natural, inborn power or quality of a thing; it referred to the *nature* of a thing. By the time Descartes had entered school, there were many interesting systems referred to as *physics*, though they mostly went by the name of *natural philosophy*. Among the more dominant systems were versions of Aristotle's physics, which are called *Aristotelian*, insofar as they were not exactly the original views of the historical Aristotle, but were inspired by and derived from his ideas. These systems typically tried to explain observed events by appealing to the powers and qualities possessed by the host of observed objects. For example, assuming that things with a common or shared nature tend to gather together, a thing with nature ***p*** will "seek out" another thing with nature ***p***. So, a rock, whose nature is constituted mostly of the element *earth*, "falls" to the ground, where the ground is simply the surface of a larger thing, whose nature is also constituted mostly of the element *earth*. A campfire, whose nature is constituted mostly of the element *fire*, "rises" to the sky, where the sky is home to a larger thing, the Sun, whose nature is also constituted mostly of the element *fire*.

An Aristotelian physics (which, remember, is not necessarily the physics of the historical Aristotle) is typically grounded in what were known as the four elements: *earth*, *fire*, *water*, and *air*. These are importantly different from the sorts of things we sense that go by the same names. The ocean, though understood to be water, is not *pure* water–that is, it isn't the element *water*. The foam present on its surface clearly shows that there is some *air* in there. The saltiness we taste indicates the presence of *earth* in there, too. The things we sense are combinations of these elements, and the variety we sense is understood as ever-complex ratios of ever-complex levels of combinations. So, wood and flesh were taken to be amazingly complex combinations of the elements.

The elements were understood in terms of two sets of contraries: *hot* and *cold*, and *wet* and *dry*. A chart of the elements might look like this:

```
                    Water
                  cold  wet
          Earth  ↗        ↘  Air
        cold  dry            hot  wet
                 ↖        ↗
                    Fire
                  hot  dry
```

The dynamism of the cosmos was accounted for by assuming that the elements were mixed up at the beginning, and they've been working their respective ways toward other elements of their kind. So, *water* is seeking *water*, *air* is seeking *air*, and so on. There are "natural" motions exhibited by the elements. Earth and water move downward (or toward the center of the cosmos), fire and air move upward (or away from center). This is why things constituted mostly of the element earth fall down toward the center of the cosmos, whereas things constituted mostly of fire rise up, away from the center of the cosmos. An Aristotelian might certainly note that things have come a long way; quite a bit of earth has come together, forming the Earth; lots of water has come together, forming oceans, rivers, and clouds; a significant quantity of air has come together, forming the atmosphere; and a large amount of fire has come together, forming the Sun. When this "seeking" like-with-like has played its way out, presumably the cosmos would look like this:

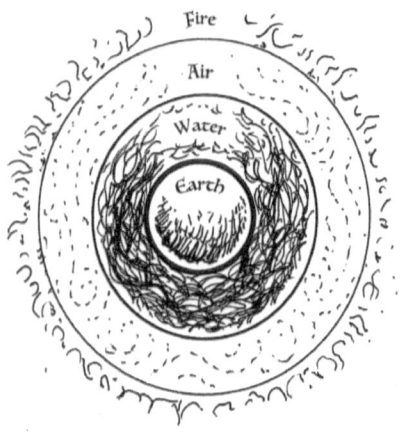

This account in part explains why the current state of things appears as it does—earth below us, air and fire above us, water around us but covering earth—and why things are always changing. This *change*, the dynamism of the cosmos, is basically the like-seeking-like process working itself out, where items *move* from one location to another, each trying to find its "natural" place.

Descartes's physics is in part a response to Aristotelian physics. In a letter to French polymath Marin Mersenne (1588-1648), he wrote that one of the aims of his *Meditations* was to destroy the principles of Aristotle's physics. (AT III 298; CSMK III 173) Therefore, Descartes specifically took on the ideas of *hot* and *cold*, with the aim of showing that there is something inherently problematic with these concepts. His analysis suggested is that any physics that bases itself on such ideas would be equally flawed. In the Third Meditation, Descartes said this about his ideas of colors, sounds, smells, tastes, and hot and cold, and the like:

> I think of these only in a very confused and obscure way, to the extent that I do not even know whether they are

true or false, that is, whether the ideas I have of them are ideas of real things or of non-things. For although, as I have noted before, falsity in the strict sense, or formal falsity, can occur only in judgments, there is another kind of falsity, material falsity, which occurs in ideas, when they represent non-things as things. For example, the ideas which I have of heat and cold contain so little clarity and distinctness that they do not enable me to tell whether cold is merely the absence of heat or vice versa, or whether both of them are real qualities, or neither is. And since there can be no ideas which are not as it were of things, if it is true that cold is nothing but the absence of heat, the idea which represents it to me as something real and positive deserves to be called false; and the same goes for other ideas of this kind. (AT VII 43-44; CSM II 30)

As we know, the only properties (modes) of body are those that presuppose extension. So, the material world is constituted at best of shaped-things of specific sizes moving about. No colors, smells, sounds, and so on, are present in the material world. They are not properties of bodies. Instead, Descartes took them to be features of the mind—an *embodied* mind's natural response to stimulus, the latter understood in terms of the motions of bodies. So, the motions of the particles that constitute what we call a *bell*, when rung, interact with the particles constituting the air, which in turn interact with the particles constituting your eardrums, which then interact with the particles constituting your inner nervous tissue (which here will include what Descartes called *animal spirits*—very fine particles), which then interact with the particles constituting the brain. By way of divine institution, specific motions in the brain trigger (occasion) specific sensory ideas—in this case, the idea of a *sound*. The *sound*, a mental artifact, represents the motions of the particles constituting the *bell*, when rung.

This was a long-standing view of Descartes's. We find it, for instance, expressed in a very early work, *The World* (c. 1629-1630). There, he said:

> Suppose we hear only the sound of some words, without attending to their meaning. Do you think the idea of this sound, as it is formed in our mind, is anything like the object which is its cause? A man opens his mouth, moves his tongue, and breathes out: I do not see anything in these actions which is not very different from the idea of the sound which they make us imagine. Most philosophers maintain that sound is nothing but a certain vibration of air which strikes our ears. Thus, if the sense of hearing transmitted to our mind the true image of its object then, instead of making us conceive the sound, it would have to make us conceive the motion of the parts of the air which is then vibrating against our ears. (AT XI 5; CSM I 82)

The idea that exhibits the *sound* instead of the motions of the air vibrating against the ears is, Descartes suggested, a *false* image. A true image would presumably be an idea that directly presented particles in motion. We could easily apply this analysis to the earlier case of our ringing the bell and hearing the resulting sound.

A view like this is also found in Descartes's more mature work. For instance, in *Description of the Human Body* (c. 1647-1648), he cast "light" as the movement of a system of tiny "balls." He noted:

> The material, as I said, is composed of many small balls which are in mutual contact; and we have sensory awareness of two kinds of motion which these balls have. One is the motion by which they approach our eyes in a straight line, which gives us the sensation of light; and the other is the motion whereby they turn about their own centers as they approach us. If the speed at which they turn is much smaller than that of their rectilinear motion, the body from which they come appears *blue* to us; while if the turning speed is

much greater than that of their rectilinear motion, the body appears *red* to us. (AT XI 255-256; CSM I 323)

Here, the idea of *blue* or *red*, it seems, would be a false image for the same reason that the idea of *sound* is a potentially misleading perception. In typical circumstances, however, these ideas, would seem to be perfectly reliable *indicators* of the activity of the bodies surrounding our own.

And the view links these two works, *The World* and *Description of the Human Body*, as we found it expressed in the passage from the Third Mediation about the materially false idea of cold. Descartes theorized later in the Sixth Meditation:

> [A]lthough I feel heat when I go near a fire and feel pain when I go too near, there is no convincing argument for supposing that there is something in the fire which resembles the heat, any more than for supposing that there is something which resembles the pain. There is simply reason to suppose that there is something in the fire, whatever it may eventually turn out to be, which produces in us the feelings of heat or pain. (AT VII 83; CSM II 57)

Related to this is something he had said a few pages earlier, when having made the proof that corporeal substance (bodies) exists:

> They may not all exist in a way that exactly corresponds with my sensory grasp of them, for in many cases the grasp of the senses is very obscure and confused. But at least they possess all the properties which I clearly and distinctly understand, that is, all those which, viewed in general terms, are comprised within the subject-matter of pure mathematics. (AT VII 80; CSM II 55)

So, it could turn out that cold is simply the absence of heat. But Descartes's discussions of sensory ideas suggest that, instead, both represent (or indicate) differences between bodies that we encounter. Let's say that you are holding an ice cube. The story here seems to be that the particles that constitute the ice cube are affecting the motions of the particles constituting your hand. Those motions then are "transferred" to the brain by way of the animal spirits (very fine particles) that fill the nerves, which, in Descartes's view, were little tubes leading to the brain. Once those motions reach the brain, certain ideas are occasioned (by way of divine institution), one of those being the idea of *cold*. Now, let's say that we put that ice cube in a pot and heat it up until it has melted and has become a steamy liquid. We pour that into our hand. Clearly, the motions of the particles constituting this steamy liquid affect the motions of the particles composing our hand differently than the motions of the particles constituting the ice cube. These motions are "transferred" to the brain, at which time certain ideas are occasioned, the relevant one here being the idea of *hot*. So, *cold* needn't be understood as a privation of *heat*, but can, instead, be perceived as representing (indicating) a certain ratio of motions holding between the particles constituting an object (the ice cube in this case) and the particles constituting your hand. We can apply a similar approach to heat: it can be understood as representing (indicating) a certain ratio of motions holding between the particles constituting an object (the steamy liquid in this case) and the particles constituting your hand.

Notice that shape, size, motion, and ratios of motion, are *mathematizable*. This is in part behind Descartes's view in the last passage quoted, that bodies, when properly understood–clearly and distinctly understood–possess those properties (modes) that fall within the domain of mathematics. In short, bodies can be subjected to mathematical description (measurement) and calculation. Now, it's important to note that Descartes was not the first to have this insight. Aristotle suggested that it could be traced back to at least Pythagoras, who had claimed that the elements of things were numbers. (*Metaphysics* 1.5 985b23-986a2) But we needn't go that far back. For example, Galileo (1564-1642), a contemporary of Descartes's, was applying mathematical description and analysis to his observations of floating bodies, falling bodies, and the like, long before Descartes published his physics (*Principles of Philosophy*). And, it is equally important to note that despite all the talk of mathematics, Descartes's physics doesn't look very mathematical. That said, some of it is. For example, he had basically described the *quantity of motion* of a thing as being equivalent to the *size* of the thing multiplied by the *speed* of the thing. (AT VIIIA 61; CSM I 240) In his *Optics*, which was published along with the *Discourse*, Descartes's treatment of light is clearly mathematical. So, there's that.

God and the Laws of Nature

Descartes's physics presupposes a number of principles that, for lack of a better term, can be called *preservation* principles. An important principle on this front, mentioned at the close of the previous section, is the preservation of the overall quantity of motion in the cosmos. The idea is that God had initially introduced some specific quantity of motion into extension, which, as suggested above, was responsible for the division of the plenum into "individuated" bodies. This specific quantity never increases nor decreases. That said, this principle is perfectly consistent with the claim that the quantity of motion increases in some region of the cosmos. Descartes sometimes referred to this as "local motion;" we might think of it as the motion of a particular body. Of course, if the motion of one body increases, there must be a proportional decrease in some other area of the cosmos, in some other body. Descartes made this clear in Part Two of the *Principles* (AT VIIIA 61; CSM I 240).

The *laws of nature*, which presuppose the preservation principles, are expressions of God's will. And, given that God's will cannot ever change (God is immutable), the laws of nature cannot change either. (*Ibid.*) Descartes established three laws of nature. They are:

First Law

Each and every thing, insofar as it can, always continues in the same state; and thus what is once in motion always continues to move

Second Law

All motion is in itself rectilinear; and hence any body moving in a circle always tends to move away from the center of the circle which it describes.

Third Law:

If a body collides with another body that is stronger than itself, it loses none of its motion; but if it collides with a weaker body, it loses a quantity of motion equal to that which it imparts to the other body.

Compare these to the three laws proposed over 40 years later by Isaac Newton (1643-1727). In his *Principia* (1687), he wrote:

First Law:

Every body preserves in its state of rest, or of uniform motion in a straight line, unless it is compelled to change that state by forces impressed thereon.

Second Law:

The alteration of motion is ever proportional to the motive force impressed; and is made in the direction of the right line in which that force is impressed.

Third Law:

To every action there is always opposed an equal reaction: or the mutual actions of two bodies upon each other are always equal, and directed to contrary parts.

Although there are significant differences here, Newton's First Law looks to incorporate some items found in Descartes's First and Second Law. Newton's Second and Third Law aimed at remedying some of the problems lurking in Descartes's Third Law. It's no secret that while he was a professor at Cambridge University (1669-1701),

Newton used Descartes's physics as a foil to his own, which means that the English scientist was familiar with Descartes's three laws.

Relatively early in his writings, Descartes adopted a form of natural philosophy that is best cast as mechanics. Such an applied mathematics had been in place for a period, no doubt traceable in some form all the way back to Archimedes. According to scholars, Descartes would've run across a version of the "mechanical philosophy" by way of his early encounters with Dutch philosopher Isaac Beekman (1588-1637). In a 1637 letter sent to poet and composer Constantijn Huygens (1596-1687), Descartes included a short discussion on machines: the pulley, the inclined plane, the wedge, the cog-wheel, the screw, and the lever. (AT I 434-447; CSMK III 66-73) This discussion, he suggested to Huygens, came, at least in part, from *The World*, a work he had pulled from the press several years before, after having heard of Galileo's troubles with church authorities. Recall from Chapter 1 that Descartes had cast his system as a tree—the roots represented *metaphysics*, the trunk *physics*, and the branches the three principal sciences—*medicine, mechanics*, and *morals*. Although his physics may look a bit like a fancy mechanics, mechanics proper is not identical to physics but is instead *grounded in* physics, and must be importantly distinct from it, in the way that a branch is distinct from the trunk. The point to stress is that Descartes took physics to describe and to explain the workings of the material world, whose fundamental nature was to be extended in length, breadth, and depth—a world of shaped things moving about or at rest. Recall that according to Descartes, in such a material world, there are no qualities such as color, smell, sound, hot and cold. These latter sorts of items were inhabitants of the mind. Although stark, this picture of the material world would prove to be quite powerful in the hands of later physicists, for it is a world of objects subject to mathematics in all the right ways.

Causation

Descartes's physics adopted primarily one kind of causation—*efficient* causation. This is best understood in light of the four kinds of cause introduced by Aristotle. In both his *Metaphysics* and *Physics*, Aristotle identified them as:

> *Formal*
> > *Material*
> > *Efficient*
> > *Final*

The formal cause of a thing accounts for the structure that the thing has, which in many cases accounts for the thing's being the kind of thing it is. The material cause of a thing accounts for the material that constitutes the thing. The efficient cause of a thing accounts for the existence of the thing. And, the final cause of a thing accounts for what the thing is for—that for the sake of which the thing exists. Consider a house. The formal cause of the house is the design (provided by the blueprints). Its material cause is traced to the materials out of which the house is built—bricks, mortar, wooden beams, and so on. The efficient cause is traced to the builders responsible for building the house—they are responsible for it being an *existent* thing. The final cause of the house is its use for shelter, shelter being that for the sake of which the house was built. We might even think of the final cause as being the *reason* for building a house.

As noted above, Descartes emphasized *efficient* causation in his system. (*Principles*, Part One, Article 28, AT VIIIA 15–16; CSM I 202) One important aim of his physics, then, is to account for the *existence* of some thing or some event (some *effect*). Why does this thing exist or why did that event occur? Descartes said almost nothing about final causation, rejecting our ability to ascertain any knowledge of final causes, since we are unable to know or understand God's aim. (*Ibid.*; also see *Principles*, Part Three, Article

2, AT VIIIA 80; CSM I 248) And, he offered no weighty discussion of either formal or material causation, leaving them to wither on the vine.

This and other models of causation familiar to Descartes and his critics run into some trouble when considering the relationship between a mind and a body. We'll explore this set of troubles in Chapter 6, which focuses on Descartes's view on human beings. So, more on causation later.

The Mechanization of Life

As with his physics, Descartes took his account of what it is to be a *living* thing to be a response to an Aristotelian account. Aristotle had thought seriously about the differences between living and non-living things. What accounts for something's being a *living* thing? Start with *matter*, the stuff from which or out of which all perceived "physical" things emerge. As we know from a previous section in this chapter, Aristotle took the most basic expressions of matter in nature to be the elements—water, fire, air, and earth. But even here, we're pretty high in the ontology, for although they were the most fundamental expressions of matter, analysis reveals that even they can be understood as being constituted of even more basic items in the ontology—the contraries hot, cold, wet, and dry. And even here we've yet to hit rock bottom. In Aristotle's view, every existing item in the cosmos ultimately was matter, the latter understood as pure potentiality, *uninformed*. This pure potentiality was brought into state of actuality, of *actual* being, when informed, the form understood as pure actuality. Matter in this deeper sense was referred to as *hyle*, whereas pure form or structure was referred to as *morphos*. A thing, an existing (individual or particular) thing in the cosmos, was a unity of *hyle* and *morphos*—a *hylomorphic* unity. And although we can (and do) speak of two items here—matter and form—the fact is that neither is completely intelligible on its own. Think, for instance, of the act of flowing. Notice that when conceiving this act, you must think of *something* that flows. That something needn't be water or lava, for example, but it must be *something*. Flowing, minus the something that flows, is unintelligible. Thus, forms minus matter (where matter is that medium which is informed) are not conceivable. So, what about this underlying matter—isn't it conceivable minus form? No. Uninformed, "matter" denotes simply pure potentiality, which is in itself not conceivable. Strip away all qualities (forms), and what you'd be left with is an idea of nothing. So, Aristotelian metaphysics is more complex than it may appear.

What makes one *kind* of thing distinct from another isn't *matter*, it isn't the "stuff" from which they emerge. In principle, all things could be constituted of the same "stuff." What makes one kind of thing distinct from another is its respective *form*, the way in which the stuff is structured or organized. So, what distinguishes the air we breathe or a piece of iron from an oak tree are their respective forms.

Living things, Aristotle claimed, were highly organized systems of matter, "organisms" that maintained a certain structure over time. A living thing takes material in from and introduces material back into the environment (respiration). A living thing is capable of reproducing others of its kind. The organizing principle is what Aristotle called the *yuch* (pronounced *pusookay*) or, when Romanized, *psyche*, from which we get the more familiar word *psychology*. The Latinists translated the Greek *psyche* as *anima*. From the latter, we get English words such as *animal* and *animation*. These etymological connections are worth keeping in mind.

When talking about the *psyche*, Aristotle took there to be three levels of organization. The first was the level at which the organism was able to maintain its structure over some period. The organism borrowed material from the environment, integrated some of it into its structure, and then discarded material back into the environment. Aristotle took plant-life to be the salient example of this level, which accounts for why it is sometimes referred to as *vegetative*. This could just as easily have been called the metabolic level, since at this point we get the account of an organism's *metabolism*. But let's say that the *psyche* goes to work to further organize something at the vegetative level, making it a more complex organism. When complex enough, this new being, Aristotle emphasized, would acquire the abilities to sense and to move. It's not surprising that this second level is sometimes referred to as the *animal* level. Things at this point continue to possess all the essential characteristics provided to beings at the vegetative level. So, animal bodies maintain their structures over time by taking in material from the environment, expelling material back into the environment, and so on. Now for the third level. When the form of an *animal* body is made even more complex through organization, a new characteristic emerges—*mind*, or the ability to *cognize*. This third level is sometimes called *rational*. In fact, Aristotle believed that the human being was essentially a *rational animal*, a being that expressed the third level of psychic organization.

When the *psyche* no longer organizes a material system, that being or organism *dies*. It ceases to be a *living* thing. A corpse is what is left after the *psyche* no longer organizes the being we previously took to be a human being.

As with his physics, Descartes's view of *life* was a response to the sort of Aristotelian view laid out above. In a very early work, *Treatise on Man* (which Descartes wrote sometime during 1629-33, but it wasn't published until 1664, 14 years after his death), he considered a thought experiment in which God makes man-like machines—what we'd today think of as *robots*. The bodies of these "men" are in principle no different from "clocks, artificial fountains, mills, and other such machines." (AT XI 120; CSM I 99) This was but one of many places where Descartes tried to explain the phenomenon philosophers refer to as *life*. We find a similar picture sketched in the Sixth Meditation. Although he rejected the notion that animals had thoughts (a mind), "I do not deny life to animals, since I regard it as consisting simply in the heat of the heart..." (1649 letter to More, AT V 278; CSMK III 366) Here, he was referring to his view that the heart is like a furnace—when it heats the blood, the heart expands, creating pressure, opening the valves on one side, in turn accounting for the circulation of blood. He contrasted his view with that of the English physician William Harvey (1578-1657), who had speculated that the heart was a pump. (see, e.g., what Descartes said in *Description of the Human Body*, AT XI 239f; CSM I 316f) Descartes's point was that the animal body was a machine.

Given this "mechanization" of life, where a "living" body was basically taken to be an "animated" machine comprised of pulleys, levers, hinges, and so on, Descartes was able to jettison the Aristotelian notion of *psyche*, as being an organizing principle of matter. He threw the notion to the side in the Second Meditation. There, he even referenced the three levels of Aristotelian organization, but drew the line at the second level. He suggested that he could appeal to matter and its specific organization to account for the first and second levels—*nourishment*, which arises in the first, and the ability to *move*, which arises in the second. His human body could be nothing more than a "mechanical structure of limbs which can be seen in a corpse, and which I called the body." (AT VII 26; CSM II 17) But thinking is different. Unlike the mechanics of a body, which presupposes *extension* (the nature of body), thinking or thought does not presuppose extension. In fact, not only does it not presume extension, but there is absolutely no intelligible relation between *thinking* and *extension*. (See what Descartes said in Article 198, Part Four of the *Principles*, AT VIIIA 322; CSM I 285.) Therefore, it will be impossible to account for *thinking* or *thought* by an appeal to body—mechanical or otherwise.

We know that Descartes took the nature of mind to be *thought* or *thinking*; the nature of body to be *extension*. There is a deep metaphysical chasm between mind and body. This distinction, as just highlighted, is made more explicit by his claim that we cannot even conceive how they *could* be related. That they are related seems pretty obvious, given our experience. But how they are related is something that we cannot ever understand. As he wrote in a letter to Princess Elisabeth of Bohemia, the primitive notion of body cannot be used to explain mind, and vice versa. "Each of them," he noted, "can be understood only through itself." (AT III 666; CSMK III 218) Even so, Descartes said that the *human being* is a *union* of mind and body. Let's now turn to our last chapter and examine some of his theories about the human being.

6. Human Beings

In Chapter 5, we learned that Descartes regarded the human being to be the *union* of a mind and body. Some scholars have wondered whether this definition would have committed Descartes to theorize that there were three kinds of substance in the cosmos: *mind*, *body*, and *human being*. Others have questioned whether Descartes might have taken the union to be not itself a substance but a special sort of *relation* between the two substances. Either way, insofar as it was a union of finite substances, the human being would *ipso facto* be real—that is, given that it is a union of substances (and even supposing that it was not itself a new substance), the union would, by that very fact, be ontologically at the level of a *real* or an *actual* thing, or, in metaphysical terms, a *substance*. The argument against the human being's being a third, independent substance—a substance that was independent of mind and body—goes as follows: Since this substance could not exist independently of either mind or body, the union couldn't be a stand-alone finite substance. In other words, the human being is not really distinct from mind or body, and therefore wouldn't itself count as a (third) finite substance. So, Descartes's take on the human being did not, in the end, challenge his mind-body dualism.

Considering, however, that human beings are really distinct from one another, they seem to fulfill the real-distinction criterion for being finite substances, at least in some qualified sense—they might be said to be finite substances in respect to each other. For, this would have some similarity to what Descartes said about God and finite mind and body. Recall that, strictly speaking, God is the only true substance. However, with respect to one another, and since mind can exist independently of body (and vice versa), we can consider them substances in some limited or qualified sense. So, maybe human beings are substances in an even more limited or qualified sense. But, as noted here, there is no consensus among scholars about what Descartes's view about this ultimately was. The good news is that regardless of how this issue is to be resolved, scholars agree that the union is special in Descartes's system. So, let's focus on the unique nature of the union.

In the Sixth Meditation we get some sense of its uniqueness:

> There is nothing that my own nature teaches me more vividly than that I have a body, and that when I feel pain there is something wrong with the body, and that when I am hungry or thirsty the body needs food and drink, and so on. So I should not doubt that there is some truth in this.
>
> Nature also teaches me, by these sensations of pain, hunger, thirst and so on, that I am not merely present in my body as a sailor is present in a ship, but that I am very closely joined and, as it were, intermingled with it so that I and the body form a unit. If this were not so, I, who am nothing but a thinking thing, would not feel pain when the body was hurt, but would perceive the damage purely by the intellect, just as a sailor perceives by sight if anything in his ship is broken. Similarly, when the body needed food or drink, I should have an explicit understanding of the fact, instead of having confused sensations of hunger and thirst. For these sensations of hunger, thirst, pain and so on are nothing but confused modes of thinking which arise from the union and, as it were, intermingling of the mind with the body. (AT VII 80-81; CSM II 56)

Here, Descartes used the Latin verb *sentio* when he meant "I feel." Although at the end of this passage he cast his sensations as confused *modes of thinking* (*cogitandi modi*), he clearly wanted to stress that this particular mode of thinking is significantly different from other modes of thinking. He didn't simply *think* that there is damage to the body, for instance, but instead, he *felt* it. The damage wasn't experienced as merely something located *in* his body, but as damage *to him*.

In the Sixth Meditation, Descartes argued that sensory

experience served to inform him of what is beneficial or harmful to the union. Sensory experience is not a reliable source for knowing anything about the nature of things, especially of material things, of things existing outside his own body. "For knowledge of the truth about such things," he noted, "seems to belong to the mind alone, not to the combination of mind and body." (AT VII 82-83; CSM II 57) This is consistent with the conclusion he had drawn in the Second Meditation after having analyzed his sensory experience of a piece of wax. There, he argued that his knowledge of the nature of body, namely that it is extended, and of its various modes such as shape, size, motion, and the like, does not originate in sensation or in imagination, but in the understanding alone; its nature is "perceived by the mind alone." (AT VII 31; CSM II 21) So long as one is clear about this, deception by way of the senses can be avoided. Even so, the senses are monumentally important to the way in which one experiences the world, and it is by paying close attention to what sensory experience teaches that one can pursue or avoid beneficial or harmful effects to the union. As we'll see shortly, this way of casting the possibility of human action allowed Descartes to develop, though only roughly, a sketch of a moral theory.

In the Sixth Set of Replies, Descartes recognized three "grades" of what he called *sensory response*:

> The first is limited to the immediate stimulation of the bodily organs by external objects; this can consist in nothing but the motion of the particles of the organs, and any change of shape and position resulting from this motion. The second grade comprises all the immediate effects produced in the mind as a result of its being united with a bodily organ which is affected in this way. Such effects include the perceptions of pain, pleasure, thirst, hunger, colors, sound, taste, smell, heat, cold and the like, which arise from the union and as it were the intermingling of mind and body, as explained in the Sixth Meditation. The third grade includes all the judgments about things outside us which we have been accustomed

to make from our earliest years—judgments which are occasioned by the movements of these bodily organs. (AT VII 436-437; CSM II 294-295)

In one sense, the first-grade sense, "sensation" refers to a motion in the body (motions of particles constituting an organ of the body, which terminate as motions in the brain). In this sense, animals and human beings can be said to have sensations.

In the second-grade sense, "sensation" refers to an idea that arises in the mind, one that the mind is immediately aware of, which is occasioned by the sensation in the first-grade sense (a motion or set of motions in the brain). Here, the idea exhibits to the mind a color, or a sound, or pain, or heat, and the like. Although this item *represents* the motions occurring in the organ or "external" object, this exhibited item certainly doesn't *resemble* those motions. Recall a passage from *Description of the Human Body* considered earlier in Chapter 5:

> The material, as I said, is composed of many small balls which are in mutual contact; and we have sensory awareness of two kinds of motion which these balls have. One is the motion by which they approach our eyes in a straight line, which gives us the sensation of light; and the other is the motion whereby they turn about their own centers as they approach us. If the speed at which they turn is much smaller than that of their rectilinear motion, the body from which they come appears *blue* to us; while if the turning speed is much greater than that of their rectilinear motion, the body appears *red* to us. (AT XI 255-256; CSM I 323)

The motions of these balls, when the balls strike our eyes, cause the particles constituting our eyes to move. Those movements are then "transferred" by the motions of the animal spirits (fine particles) that inhabit the nerves (which are little tubes). The motions reach the interior of the brain. At this point—though it's not clear whether the presence of these movements in the interior of the brain is enough to trigger an idea on their own, or whether they must produce some change (in motion) in the pineal gland or in a pattern of motion on the gland's surface—an idea in the mind is occasioned. This (the idea) is what the mind is immediately aware of. The connection between a specific set of motions and a specific set of ideas is divinely instituted (perhaps expressed in the form of *rules*, as noted earlier). The idea of which the mind is aware, having been created in the fashion just described, is a sensation in the second-grade sense. In this sense, animals cannot be said to have sensations, since, in Descartes's view, they are merely corporeal beings, and do not have minds.

It also seems to be the case that disembodied minds—minds not united to a body—do not have sensations in the second-grade sense. In a letter to the Dutch physician Henricus Regius (1598-1679), Descartes wrote that the perception of sensations (*sensation* in the second-grade sense) are not possible thoughts of a mind minus union, but are "confused perceptions of a mind really united to a body." (January 1642 letter to Regius, AT III 493; CSMK III 206) Even so, not just any finite mind when "occupying" a body will have sensations in the second-grade sense; even if an angel, the paradigm of a disembodied mind, were to occupy the body of a man, "he would not have sensations as we do, but would simply perceive the motions which are caused by external objects, and in this way would differ from a real man." (*Ibid.*) The mind of *man* is special in that its relation to body, when "embodied," is *sui generis*, which means "unique." Nothing else is like it.

Death, as Descartes opined in *The Passions of the Soul* (1649), comes to a human being upon the cessation of bodily function. (AT XI 330-331; CSM I 329) As a result, the soul (the mind) "takes its leave." (*Ibid.*) The body doesn't function because the mind is in union with it. Rather, he said, there is some corporeal principle that accounts for the movements of all its parts, as designed by God. (AT XI 331; CSM I 329) Our bodies, according to Descartes, are like watches that have been properly wound. They run their course as they "wind down." Once completely unwound, whatever had been in place to keep the movements going is now gone. In the Synopsis of the *Meditations*, Descartes had suggested a possible argument for the immortality of the mind. As we now know, the nature of body is extension. It is (modally) divisible by its very nature. A particular body is corrupted, recall, by way of division and scattering. This is different from annihilation, which requires God to withdraw His concurrence. Presumably, then, the *human* body is corrupted by division—the parts "break down," or, as Descartes explained, they *decay*. The mind, by contrast, is not extended. Therefore, it cannot be divided or corrupted. Although Descartes admitted that this conclusion only suggests the immortality of the mind (soul), he thought it was a pretty good argument. (AT VII 13-14; CSM II 9-10)

So, what might it be like to be a disembodied human mind? As interesting as this question may sound, it isn't properly formed. For starters, there would be no disembodied *human* minds, given that a human mind is in union with a body. This question might be better formulated like this: what is it like to be a disembodied mind that was once embodied? Descartes didn't have much to say about this. But, what little he did proffer on this subject is interesting. For instance, he seemed to have held that there are at least two kinds of memory: *intellectual* and *corporeal*. The first kind doesn't require a body at all, whereas the second does. This latter kind of memory has its origin in the brain, where "traces" of the motions are kept for some time. Those traces can be stimulated and as a result, can occasion certain ideas to arise in the mind. In a letter to poet Huygens, Descartes posited:

> Those who die pass to a sweeter and more tranquil life than ours; I cannot imagine otherwise. We shall go to find them some day, and we shall still remember the past; for we have, in my view, an intellectual memory which is certainly independent of the body. (10 October 1642 letter, AT III 598; CSMK III 216)

In another letter, to his friend Denis Mesland (1616-1672), Descartes wrote:

> As for memory, I think that the memory of material things depends on the traces which remain in the brain after an image has been imprinted on it; and that the memory of intellectual things depends on some other traces which remain in the mind itself. But the latter are of a wholly different kind from the former, and I cannot explain them by any illustration drawn from corporeal things without a great deal of qualification. (2 May 1644 letter, AT IV 114; CSMK III 233)

So, the mind can have "traces" too. As Descartes noted here, it would be difficult to explain what those traces amount to. The view seems to be that a previously embodied but currently disembodied mind would still be able to recall some things from its embodied life, though those things would be purely intellectual. This means that such memories would not be corporeal in nature—they wouldn't be *extended images*, for instance, of places one had visited, or of faces of loved ones. The experience of a disembodied mind that was once embodied, it seems, would be very much like the mind of an angel.

One "picture" of an embodied mind, Descartes suggested, is the image one has of one's own body. (28 June 1643 Letter to Elisabeth, AT III 691; CSMK III 226) Much later, Cambridge philosopher Ludwig Wittgenstein (1889-1951) wrote something similar: "The human body is the best picture of the human soul." (*Philosophical Investigations*, Part II, iv, 178e) Such a picture is easily formed by reflecting on one's own sensory experience—a reflection showing that the mind and body are a unit. For, if you are pricked with a needle, you feel the prick, and if you want to extend your hand, the hand moves. According to Descartes, ordinary folks who have no knowledge of philosophy "regard both [mind and body] as a single thing, that is to say, they conceive their union..." (AT III 692; CSMK III 227) Even when we think of ourselves, or speak about ourselves (which was Wittgenstein's point), as *disembodied* souls (minds) existing in the afterlife, we are forced to imagine ourselves in no other form than in that of our own bodies, as they appeared while living. This picture, as noted, seems to have its origin in sensory experience. When properly instructed, however, Descartes said that people could be shown how to employ their intellectual ability to understand the nature of the mind—which is to think. The nature of body, by contrast, can be understood by way of the intellect, but things are much clearer if one employs the imagination. Forming the clearest conception of the union, however, is actually best determined by sensory experience, and not by the pure intellect or the imagination. (*Ibid.*) Descartes's view was that although we are convinced of a union of mind and body, there is no way to *understand* how they are united. Our conviction is rooted in our sensory *experience* of the union.

In the Sixth Meditation, Descartes made it clear that his sensory experience had two components. The first is the obvious one, which is immediately exhibited to him—namely the experience of some quality such as color, or sound, or heat, and the like. For Descartes, this was an ideal component: a mode of the mind. Now, the other component, whatever that may be, is the impetus or the origin of the ideational component. It's what is responsible for bringing this particular idea to mind. There are at least two possible candidates for this second component: Descartes's own mind or something that isn't Descartes's mind. If it is his mind, it must be his *will*, which, we learned in previous chapters, is the principal companion faculty to the intellect, the intellect being that faculty to which we trace the occurring idea. So, we might ask: to which faculty do we assign the exhibiting of our ideas? And, the answer will be: the intellect or understanding. This faculty, Descartes suggested, is passive. The active component of thought is associated with the faculty of the *will*. This can be what accounts for the intellect bringing an idea to the mind—for example, when you *want* to think of a triangle. The will is the faculty responsible for the intellect's producing this idea before the mind.

In light of this, Descartes argued:

> Now there is a passive faculty of sensory perception, that is,

a faculty for receiving and recognizing the ideas of sensible objects; but I could not make use of it unless there was also an active faculty, either in me or in something else, which produced or brought about these ideas. But this faculty cannot be in me, since clearly it presupposes no intellectual act on my part, and the ideas in question are produced without my cooperation and often even against my will. So the only alternative is that it is in another substance distinct from me—a substance with contains either formally or eminently all the reality which exists objectively in the ideas produced by this faculty (as I have just noted). (AT VII 79; CSM II 55)

The ideas produced in sensory experience were not only exhibited to him without his cooperation, but they came even *against* his will. So, unlike the idea of the triangle, the will could not be the agent responsible for bringing about *these* ideas. Instead, the agent must be some other substance that is distinct from his own mind. Why can't this other substance be another mind? It cannot because the thing responsible for producing this particular class of ideas must ultimately be extended, shaped, in motion, and so on. For, if it isn't ultimately a substance with these characteristics, God, who instituted in us our spontaneous impulse to believe that the things causing in us such ideas are bodies, would be a deceiver. We discussed this in some detail in Chapter 4, so we won't dwell on those details here. The point to stress is that the agent-substance responsible for bringing about the ideas of sensory experience is a body—a substance whose nature is to be extended. To be sure, this conclusion is reached by way of an argument, and so is a product of reason, but that doesn't count against Descartes's insistence that sensory experience is the best and clearest avenue to "understand" the union. The argument serves to support our ordinary sensory experience. So, the view is that if you are essentially a mind, you are nevertheless, in being human, intimately united with a body (or with some region of *res extensa*).

In an odd piece titled *Comments on a Certain Broadsheet* (1648), Descartes argued that even the *ideas* of motion, pain, color, sound, and so on, are *innate* in the mind. (AT VIIIB 359; CSM I 304) Some scholars have found the remark perplexing, given Descartes's insistence in other places that there are three (maybe four) innate ideas–the ideas of God, finite mind, body (and maybe union). The *Broadsheet* was written as a response to things publicly claimed by his friend Regius, who, you may recall, was the correspondent related to Descartes's talk about the angel occupying the body of a man. In the *Broadsheet*, Descartes was likely referring to an *embodied* mind of a human being. Even so, his remarks are consistent with what he said about disembodied minds as they exist independently of body. The challenge is in figuring out what he meant by *innate*. As we know from Chapter 2, Descartes believed that the ideas of God and body are innate, but also argued that they have their origin in God and body, respectively. In this sense, they look a lot like what he called *adventitious* ideas, such as the sensory idea of the Sun. For, the adventitious idea of the Sun has its origin in (the formal reality of) the Sun. In the *Broadsheet*, the ideas that would in other contexts be cast as sensory (or even as adventitious) are now cast as innate. So, what's going on here? Although it's not perfectly clear, we might find help by considering something Descartes said to Thomas Hobbes (1588-1679), the author of the Third Set of Objections. In the Third Set of Replies Descartes wrote:

> When we say that an idea is innate in us, we do not mean that it is always there before us. This would mean that no idea was innate. We simply mean that we have within ourselves the faculty for summoning up the idea. (AT VII 189; CSM II 132)

So, perhaps in the *Broadsheet* Descartes meant that a finite (human) mind has the *capacity* to have ideas such as the ideas of motion, color, sound, and the like. This is consistent with his saying that in some cases the ideas are "triggered" by the *will*, while other ideas are "triggered" by (one's being united with) *body*.

The Problem of Mind-Body Interaction

Princess Elisabeth of Bohemia raised the following concern to Descartes, in a letter dated 6 May 1643:

> So I ask you please to tell me how the soul of a human being (it being only a thinking substance) can determine the bodily spirits, in order to bring about voluntary actions. For it seems that all determination of movement happens through the impulsion of the thing moved, by the manner in which it is pushed by that which moves it, or else by the particular qualities and shape of the surface of the latter. Physical contact is required for the first two conditions, extension for the third. You entirely exclude the one [extension] from the notion you have of the soul, and the other [physical contact] appears to me incompatible with an immaterial thing. (AT III 660; Shapiro 62)

This is a powerful criticism. Assuming that causal interaction requires the possibility of contact, then this kind of interplay between bodies is at least possible. How so? Well, bodies have surfaces (*via* their having shapes), and it is by way of their surfaces that bodies can "touch" one another—they can come into contact. We know that in Descartes's view, shape presupposes extension. All shaped things are extended. Conversely, all finitely extended things have some shape or other. So far so good. But what about mind? As we also know, and as Elisabeth rightly said, Descartes theorized that the nature of mind is *thinking* or *thought*, and that, as he noted in the Synopsis of the *Meditations*, mind and body "are not only different, but in some way opposite." (AT VII 13; CSM II 10) Their being contraries is emphasized in the Sixth Meditation:

on the one hand I have a clear and distinct idea of myself, in so far as I am simply a thinking, non-extended thing; and on the other hand I have a distinct idea of body, in so far as this is simply an extended, non-thinking thing. (AT VII 78; CSM II 54)

So, the mind is not extended. What follows from this? For starters, if the mind isn't extended, it cannot be shaped. This amounts to saying that it won't have a surface. And, if it doesn't have a surface, *contact* is rendered impossible (unintelligible). Therefore, as Elisabeth's criticism affirms, there would be no way for a mind and body to engage in causal interaction—or, perhaps more accurately, there would be no way for us to conceive such interaction. And if this were the case, then despite what sensory experience suggests, the mind and body *could not* form a unit—or, at the very least, we would be at a loss when trying to understand how such a unit could be formed. Descartes's reply focused on the latter, that is, on our inability to clearly *understand* the union of mind and body. That they form a unit, he continued to insist, is confirmed in sensory experience. His exchange with Elisabeth on this subject inspired Descartes to write what would turn out to be his final work—*The Passions of the Soul*. In part, the *Passions* was intended to address some of Elisabeth's concerns. Let's have a brief look at this work before bringing this chapter (and this book!) to a close.

Passions and Virtue: The Makings of a Moral Theory

Descartes said very little about moral theory, and almost nothing about political theory. In the *Passions*, he discussed his take on virtue, on happiness, and the like, and did more than to suggest the makings of a moral theory. In this section, we'll examine his view about the possibility of moral (or right) action.

Prior to the *Passions*, Descartes had been corresponding with Elisabeth about right action. He discussed his take on Seneca's *On the Happy Life* in a series of letters, drawing some connections between it and his own view. In this work, Seneca considered the view of the Greek philosopher Epicurus, which Descartes understood to be the following: The structure of human action depicts the embodied mind as aiming ultimately for happiness, which to Descartes meant *contentment* of mind. This is the goal or payoff of human action. As he put it in a letter to Elisabeth, it is the *prize*. (AT IV 277; CSMK III 262) But this prize, the attainment of which is the ultimate goal, must be won. How is it won? According to the analogy he employed, it is won by hitting the bulls-eye. Virtue, he said, is the bulls-eye (*Ibid.*) By wanting to win the prize, one will be compelled to hit the bulls-eye—where hitting the bulls-eye is to be virtuous. He argued that if one were not aware of the prize, and were only aware of the bulls-eye (being virtuous), one would not be compelled to be virtuous (for, one might not see the *point* in hitting the bulls-eye). Although not clear, this view that he took from Seneca was likely consistent with his own.

Earlier in this letter, Descartes wrote:

> My first observation [of what Seneca says] is that there is a difference between happiness, the supreme good, and the final end or goal towards which our actions ought to tend. For happiness is not the supreme good, but presupposes it, being the contentment or satisfaction of the mind which results from possessing it. The end of our actions, however, can be understood to be one or the other; for the supreme good is undoubtedly the thing we ought to set ourselves as the goal of all our actions, and the resulting contentment of the mind is also rightly called our end, since it is the attraction which makes us seek the supreme good. (AT IV 275; CSMK III 261)

What Descartes said in the above passage is not clear. One way to read this is that Descartes suggested that happiness isn't identical with the supreme good, but is instead presupposed in the supreme good. So, in aiming to win the supreme good, one is, by that very fact, aiming to win (possess) happiness. Another way to decipher this is that Descartes is saying that happiness presupposes the supreme good. So, in pursuing happiness one is, by that very fact, pursuing the supreme good. Either way, virtue is brought into play in our pursuing some end.

In an earlier letter, Descartes noted that "the greatest happiness of man depends on the right use of reason." (AT IV 267; CSMK III 258) This is directly related, he suggested, to the moral rules he had put forward in the *Discourse*:

- *One should always try to employ one's mind as well as one can to discover what one should or should not do in all of life's circumstances.*
- *One should have a firm and constant resolution to carry out whatever reason recommends without being diverted by one's passions or appetites.*
- *One should always bear in mind the difference between those things that fall within one's power to possess (or control) and those things that fall outside one's power—so that one learns to only desire the former.*

These are summaries of the first three maxims introduced in the *Discourse* (there is a fourth, but he didn't mention it in the letter). Virtue, he said, is expressed in the second rule above: Virtue "consists precisely in sticking firmly to this resolution." (*Ibid.*) This appears to vary from his metaphor about hitting the bulls-eye, where the prize is happiness. So, perhaps this is where Descartes's view differs from the one expressed by Epicurus. Difficult to say.

The view seems to be that the intellect presents some good, and the virtuous will is that which "chooses" to pursue or is "resolute" in pursuing this good. So, virtue isn't the *pursuing*, but the *choosing* to pursue the good. Like Plato, Descartes also seemed to believe that the intellect is key since it must be up to the task of presenting a genuine good. For, if one's intellect is deficient, or one is ignorant, what one's intellect presents may turn out to be a harm. Even so, one would act virtuously if one were resolute in pursuing what the intellect presents as the good. This allows for the ironic possibility of the virtuous person doing evil things (things that are not in one's best interest). For, an ignorant person may believe something to be good, may be resolute to pursue what is presented as good (and thus be virtuous), but because the presented good is not really good, this person does what in fact is bad—he or she does something *evil*. (AT IV 267; CSMK III 258) To rule out this possible irony, Descartes referred to the kind of "virtue" exhibited by the ignorant person as *false* virtue. (*Ibid.*) To counter false virtue, one must do one's best to be knowledgeable about things, which is expressed in the first moral rule listed above. This, as just noted, appears to be similar to Plato's view.

In an even earlier letter to Elisabeth, Descartes wrote that *perfect health* "is the foundation of all the other goods in this life." (AT IV 220; CSMK III 250) He later cast *health* and *illness* as a *good* and an *evil* respectively. Good health, given his remarks considered earlier, would presuppose the supreme good, which, as he also claimed, would presuppose happiness. Recalling what he said in the Sixth Meditation, the senses serve as a means to inform the mind of what is beneficial and harmful to the union. That is their primary function. So, the senses will play an important role in Descartes's moral theory.

Now, a *passion* of the soul (mind) is this: a *thought* that is brought about by some occurring motion or set of motions in the brain. This thought can remain so long as the occasioning motion(s) is (are) present in the brain. A passion is understood as such in light of its counterpart, a correlated *action*. The active component here is the aforementioned motion(s). Therefore, Descartes said that it is best to understand the pairing—action/passion—as a *single* item. (AT XI 328; CSM I 328) The principal effect of the passions "is that they move and dispose the soul to want the things for which they prepare the body. Thus, the feeling of fear moves the soul to want to flee, that of courage to want to fight, and similarly with the others." (AT XI 359; CSM I 343) Note here that he referred to the experience of a passion as a *feeling* (he used the French word, *sentiment*). So, we might classify the passions as emotions.

In Chapter 2, we considered Malebranche's version of Cartesian philosophy. Recall that Malebranche postulated two fundamental faculties or capacities, the *understanding* and the *will*. The former was the capacity to receive ideas. It was cast as a passive element of cognition. The faculty of the will, on the other hand, was the capacity to act. It was cast as an active element of cognition. From the faculty of the will arises an "impulse," which, Malebranche argued, directed the mind toward goodness in general. This sounds close to Descartes's view. That said, Malebranche identified God as goodness in general. The mind's impulse is by its very nature directed at God, toward the "infinite," for in encompassing all *possible* "terminal points," the will cannot but tend toward God. This is true of all volitions. From the faculty of the understanding arises an *idea*. This represents a particular good. The impulse can be subsequently redirected to this. By choosing diverse ideas, the mind sets the stage for the various particulars that it can desire, though ultimately the desire for God is ever-present since any particular good will presuppose goodness in general. According to Malebranche, choosing that to which the impulse is directed (which is another way of saying that one is directing the impulse to a particular good) is *freedom*.

Recall also from Chapters 2 and 3 that Descartes took clear and distinct ideas to *compel* the will. If such an idea is present, the will is drawn to it. This, Descartes said, would be an example of freedom in its strongest sense:

> In order to be free, there is no need for me to be inclined both ways; on the contrary, the more I incline in one direction—either because I clearly understand that reasons of truth and goodness point that way, or because of a divinely produced disposition of my inmost thoughts—the

> freer is my choice...But the indifference I feel when there is no reason pushing me in one direction rather than another is the lowest grade of freedom; it is evidence not of any perfection of freedom, but rather of a defect in knowledge or a kind of negation. (AT VII 57-58; CSM II 40)

If the will isn't compelled to assent, then one isn't really "free," or if we still want to call the state of indifference or that of a "frozen" will *freedom*, it will only be "freedom" in the weakest sense. We know that in Descartes's view God has instituted in the union, *via* the senses, some acquaintance with what is beneficial and harmful. So, the senses are good resources for acting in the world. The feeling of pain will urge us to avoid, while the feeling of pleasure will urge us to pursue. Even so, since the senses are not the salient faculties for acquiring the truth of things, they cannot be given the final word on moral action. For instance, although having your teeth cleaned may be slightly uncomfortable, or even a bit painful, and one's natural disposition would be to avoid such a thing, the understanding may present to you the "long-term" benefit of having your teeth cleaned. Exhibiting to you the great "long-term" benefit in having your teeth cleaned may help you override this otherwise natural disposition to avoid having your teeth cleaned. You understand that this temporary and slight discomfort is outweighed by the pleasure you will experience in having sound oral health.

Descartes's sketch of moral action is *teleological*. That is, it is goal-directed, where the aim is to acquire or attain happiness (contentment). In this way, concern about an Aristotelian *final* cause is back on the table. But, as we know from earlier discussions, Descartes insisted that an understanding of "morals" requires an understanding of his physics. (See, for example, what he said in the Synopsis of the *Meditations*, AT VII 13-14; CSM II 10, and in the Preface to the French edition of the *Principles*, AT IXB 14-15; CSM I 186) And, an understanding of the physics will not include reference to any end or aim, since, as Descartes also insisted, it is not possible to know the end or goal that God had in mind when creating the cosmos. (AT VIIIA 15-16; CSM I 202, AT VIIIA 80-81; CSM I 248-249) But perhaps the connection to the physics is with the underlying preservation principles. Recall that God introduces a certain quantity of motion into the cosmos, where that quantity has persevered. It never increases or decreases. Although Descartes never mentioned it, perhaps he thought that since God had introduced the union of mind and body, *via* Adam and Eve, say, it might follow that to work toward eliminating such a thing from the inventory of the cosmos would work against God's initial plan, as revealed in Holy Scripture. This might explain why one is *obligated* to act in a way that preserves one's union. But figuring out whether this was Descartes's view is difficult, and there is no consensus among scholars about even the basics of a moral theory in Descartes's writings. That said, it should be clear that the basics of a moral theory are lurking in his writings.

Let's close this chapter with one final case, where we'll piece together the basics of what Descartes posited in the *Passions* and in certain letters. Suppose that you walk into the palace and see the Queen. You are immediately drawn to her. Let's call this "drawing" an expression of *lust*. So, you lust after the Queen. A Cartesian explanation of this might go as follows: certain motions originating with the surface of the Queen's body are communicated *via* the medium called *light* and affect the motions of the particles constituting your eyeballs. Those motions are "transmitted" to the interior cavity of your brain, through the animal spirits that occupy your nerves. These motions occasion the idea that represents the Queen as a *good* object—she is the object of your desire. These motions also trigger certain bodily responses. So, you find that independently of your will, your legs begin to move your body in her direction. Your heart pounds, your breathing becomes rapid, your hands begin to sweat. You really *want* the Queen. Now, as you move, you see the King out of the corner of your eye. Immediately the thought of his divining your intentions and having you executed comes to mind. That stops you dead (no pun intended) in your tracks.

What has happened is that this thought, the thought of being executed, has overtaken the pineal gland, and is keeping it at bay, which is also why your legs stopped moving. This thought exhibits a greater "force" on the gland than the motions originating with the Queen's body, the motions that occasioned the idea of the Queen as object of desire, and so on. (AT XI 364-366; CSM I 346-347) If you let the thought of execution go, the motions that got you initially moving will be free to again influence you, and you'll resume your lustful march toward the Queen. Keep that thought of execution in mind, however, and the march is stopped. What do you do? Virtuous action here would arise from your being resolute to pursue that which preserves the union. The thought of your being executed stops you from making a move on the Queen, it will preserve the union in this case. Since this is so, the virtuous thing to do is to choose let this thought remain before the mind, so that it can "overcome" the feeling of lust initially produced. For, pursuing your lust will surely put an end to your union. If you're familiar with ethical theories, this should remind you of an early form of consequentialism, or even an early form of utilitarianism, where such views basically say that the good is to be found in the outcome or consequences of our actions, where the *right* action is the one that will maximize the good. There are versions of these theories that emphasize an egocentric goal, where the right action is the one that maximizes one's own good. This sounds a bit like Descartes's view, where the right action is the one that will preserve the union, which is one's own good.

So, we have journeyed from an account of Descartes's metaphysics, including discussions of the two principal finite substances—mind and body—through a brief explanation of his physics and "biology," to his account of the human being and the possibility of moral agency. The Cartesian system is wonderful and rich, a system which we know had a real impact on the development of "Western" thinking. And now you know of it too.

7. Descartes's Legacy

Using powerful university search-engines, the evidence suggests that there isn't a single year this millennium (or, in fact, in the last century) in which we cannot find something published on Descartes or on some of his views. We're not talking just scholarly bits either—but everyday, ordinary pieces in popular, commercial publications. For example, as recently as 2017 in *The Stone*, which is part of the *Opinions* section of *The New York Times*, we find Christia Mercer's letter of September 25, 2017, titled "Descartes Is Not Our Father." Of course, Mercer is an eminent philosophy professor at Columbia University, so you might not count that as "popular" writing (but in this case, it is!). We find similar pieces in *Browsings: The Harper's blog*, of *Harper's* magazine; such as Scott Horton's 2010 piece, "Descartes–The Chain of Reason." There are also many book reviews, including, for instance, a 2017 Thomas Nagel review of Daniel Dennett's book, *From Bacteria to Bach and Back: The Evolution of Minds* (Norton, 2017), which can be found in *The New Yorker*.

But it shouldn't go unnoticed that ordinary folks have been entertained by screenwriters who have twisted Descartes's view here or there to produce wonderful films—*The Matrix*, *The Truman Show*, *Inception*, to name only three. There is the 1974 film by Italian director Roberto Rossellini, *Cartesius*, which purports to chronicle Descartes's life. But it's not for everyone. In graduate school, my friends and I used to turn off the volume and subtitles and enjoy making up our own dialogue, which I must admit got quite saucy. So, there's that.

But good and bad movies aside, each semester droves of college freshmen are formally introduced to Descartes in their introductory philosophy courses by way of their reading and discussing his *Mediations* (well, usually just the First and Second Meditation, and sometimes the Sixth) or his *Discourse*. This practice has been going on at least since the late 1800s. Even earlier, Isaac Newton taught some of Descartes's physics in his classes at Cambridge; as with so many others, he did this not to teach Descartes's physics, but to show where it fails. In fact, it would not be an exaggeration to say that many college freshmen are exposed to versions of Descartes's views in disciplines outside of philosophy, such as in math, psychology, cognitive science, and neuroscience—not because his views are thought to be right (at least they are not as these various disciplines understand Descartes's theories), but because the doctrines that are now thought to be right are understood to be so in light of how they show his to be wrong. Ironically, Descartes's popularity can in part be explained by the fact that generations of thinkers following in his wake continue to bring him up in order to show that something he said was incorrect. But perhaps he won't play the role of proverbial foil forever. I just caught a recent episode of the television show *Ancient Aliens* in which Descartes's mind-body dualism was offered as possible support for the view that human bodies are like "robots," which, when properly functioning, can support communication with otherwise independently existing minds, where the latter needn't exist "here" or "there" on earth.

But fun television shows aside, Descartes's legacy is found in mathematics, where he had the insight to relate Euclidean geometry and algebra, and published this in *The Geometry*. As far as I am aware, not a single thing he said in that work has ever been shown to be false. No doubt mathematicians following in Descartes's wake named the now-familiar x-y coordinate system after him—the *Cartesian Coordinate System*. Not only did his thinking that living bodies were machine-like have a great impact on the evolution of medicine, but his mind-body dualism has been the source of much scholarly debate in recent years. Several papers appear in journals that link the latter to issues of patient treatment, and most notably issues in psychiatric treatment (see, for example, Jeffery Gold's "Cartesian dualism and the current crisis in medicine—a plea for a philosophical approach: discussion paper" in *Journal of the Royal Society of Medicine*, Vol. 78, August 1985, pp. 663-66; or

Michael Sharpe and Jane Walker's "Mind-body dualism, psychiatry, and medicine," in *New Oxford Textbook of Psychiatry*, Second Edition, Oxford: Oxford University Press, 2012).

It should be clear that Descartes, for good or ill, has had a significant impact on you and me—whether we realize it or not. The books in this Simply Charly series, which bring to the general reader a better understanding of individuals who have had a significant impact on our lives, in whatever fields they worked, are of great importance, since they help us comprehend where we come from which, in turn, can help us navigate where we believe we ought to go from here. Paraphrasing something that I often heard as a kid: you can't know where you're going unless you know where you've been. Descartes's legacy, even ignoring all the things brought to light in this book, is that his insights, whether right or wrong, continue to help us advance our wonderful and noble species closer to that more perfect expression of what it is to be human.

Suggested Reading

Since Descartes's death in 1650, much has been published concerning his philosophical views; most of the earliest publications were understandably not in English. Descartes wrote almost exclusively in Latin—though some of his important works, the *Discourse*, for instance, originally appeared in French and was later translated into Latin. His writings suffered some setbacks with respect to public access, being put on the *Index* in 1663—a Catholic list of prohibited books. Adrien Baillet published *La vie de Monsieur Des-Cartes* (*The Life of Mr. Descartes*), in two volumes, in 1691. There are some books published in the latter half of the 19th century that include excerpts of Descartes's work, at least one in English, but perhaps the best place to locate Descartes's original writings are in a collection that Charles Adam and Paul Tannery put together, which is now considered the *standard* in terms of collections; there are 11 volumes, including five volumes of correspondence. This collection was published by J. Vrin as *Oeuvres de Descartes* in 1897. These texts are mostly in Latin and in French, though some letters can be found written in Dutch. In 2003, Theo Verbeek, Erik-Jan Bos, and Jeroen Van de Ven, reacting to problems they found lurking in the Adam and Tannery's ordering of certain letters, reworked some of the correspondence in *The Correspondence of René Descartes 1643*. And around 2012 or so, Descartes's correspondence was made available online, in *Early Modern Letters Online* (EMLO), which can be accessed here:

http://emlo-portal.bodleian.ox.ac.uk/collections/?catalogue=rene-descartes

The above-mentioned sources are probably better suited for scholars doing research than for the general reader who simply wants to learn more about Descartes's life and views. Fortunately, much has been written in English on those topics, and these books are better suited for the general reader, especially for the English reader, who can be spared having to learn Latin.

As biographies go, aside from Baillet's, mentioned above, many people find Tom Sorell's *Descartes* (Oxford University Press, 1987), John Cottingham's *Descartes* (Oxford University Press, 1998), and Genevieve Rodis-Lewis's *Descartes: His Life and Thought* (Cornell University Press, 1999), the latter now available in English, easy reading and very helpful. Richard Watson's *Cogito Ergo Sum: The Life of René Descartes* (Godine, 2007) is a good, colorful, and delightful read. There are several online sources, too. For example, there is Gary Hatfield's "René Descartes," in *The Stanford Encyclopedia of Philosophy*, and my own "Descartes' Life and Works" in *The Stanford Encyclopedia of Philosophy*, which can be accessed online here:

https://plato.stanford.edu/entries/descartes/
https://plato.stanford.edu/entries/descartes-works/

Works focused on Descartes's views are too numerous to list here. They not only include books, websites, and online encyclopedias, but a host of articles published in scholarly journals, in many languages. But we might narrow things down if we list just those works published in English that have had a palpable influence on Descartes scholarship. There is Martial Gueroult's two-volume work, originally published in French in 1952, *Descartes' Philosophy Interpreted According to the Order of Reasons*; it was translated into English and published in 1984 (University of Minnesota Press, 1984). There is also Anthony Kenny's *Descartes: A Study of His Philosophy* (Thoemmes Press, 1968). Several excellent books appeared in 1978: Bernard Williams' *Descartes: The Project of Pure Enquiry* (Penguin Books); Margaret Wilson's *Descartes* (Routledge & Kegan Paul); and Edwin Curley's *Descartes Against the Skeptics* (Basil Blackwell). Then there are books focused primarily on Descartes's natural philosophy, such as Daniel Garber's *Descartes' Metaphysical Physics* (University of Chicago Press, 1992) and Dennis Des Chene's *Spirits and Clocks: Machine and Organism in Descartes* (Cornell University Press, 2001). A very good and concise account of Descartes's physics can be found in Edward Slowik's "Descartes' Physics," in *The Stanford Encyclopedia of Philosophy*. The URL is:

https://plato.stanford.edu/entries/descartes-physics/

And, there are books specifically focused on Descartes's views on mind and his mind-body dualism: Desmond Clarke's *Descartes's Theory of Mind* (Oxford University Press, 2003), Lilli Alanen's *Descartes's Concept of Mind* (Harvard University Press, 2003), Deborah Brown's *Descartes and the Passionate Mind* (Cambridge University Press, 2006), and Marleen Rozemond's *Descartes's Dualism* (Harvard University Press, 1998). An insightful and productive amalgam of biography and views is Stephen Gaukroger's *Descartes: An Intellectual Biography* (Clarendon Press, 1995). Numerous scholarly books are focused on Descartes's mathematics, but probably the best way to ease into this body of literature is to look first at Mary Domski's "Descartes' Mathematics," in *The Stanford Encyclopedia of Philosophy*. The URL is:

https://plato.stanford.edu/entries/descartes-mathematics/

In the bibliography of Domski's entry, the reader will find a solid list of books focused on Descartes's mathematics.

Several books geared for general readers, both non-fiction and fiction, have emerged that are entertaining and informative–though admittedly, even the non-fiction here is speculative, based on testimony, rumor, and circumstantial evidence. One such book is Russell Shorto's *Descartes' Bones: A Skeletal History of the Conflict Between Faith and Reason* (Vintage, 2009), in which we learn, among other things, the story of Descartes's remains being brought back to France; another is A. C. Grayling's *Descartes: The Life and Times of a Genius* (Walker Books, 2006), which suggests the existence of evidence pointing to Descartes's being a spy! A fun and provocative novel is Andrew Pessin's *The Irrationalist: The Tragic Murder of René Descartes* (Open Books, 2017), which, as the title suggests, pieces together the possible murder of Descartes under the employ of Queen Christina.

About the Author

Kurt Smith is Professor of Philosophy at Bloomsburg University of Pennsylvania. He earned his BA at UC Irvine, and his MA and Ph.D. in philosophy at Claremont Graduate University. He is the author of *Matter Matters: Metaphysics and Methodology in the Early Modern Period* (2010) and has written numerous articles and contributed to books focused on Descartes and the modern period. He is currently working on a book about various conceptions of the unconscious as they emerged in the modern period.

A Word from the Publisher

Thank you for reading *Simply Descartes*!

If you enjoyed reading it, we would be grateful if you could help others discover and enjoy it too.

Please review it with your favorite book provider such as Amazon, BN, Kobo, Apple Books, or Goodreads, among others.

Again, thank you for your support and we look forward to offering you more great reads.

www.ingramcontent.com/pod-product-compliance
Lightning Source LLC
Chambersburg PA
CBHW020141130526
44591CB00030B/169